craft **workshop**

machine embroidery

The art of creative stitchery in 25 innovative projects

Isabel Stanley

photography by Peter Williams

southwater

THIS EDITION IS PUBLISHED BY SOUTHWATER

SOUTHWATER IS AN IMPRINT OF ANNESS PUBLISHING LTD
HERMES HOUSE, 88–89 BLACKFRIARS ROAD, LONDON SE1 8HA
TEL. 020 7401 2077; FAX 020 7633 9499

© ANNESS PUBLISHING LTD 1996, UPDATED 2002

011803238

PUBLISHED IN THE USA BY
SOUTHWATER
ANNESS PUBLISHING INC.
27 WEST 20TH STREET, NEW
YORK, NY 10011
FAX 212 807 6813

THIS EDITION DISTRIBUTED IN
THE UK BY THE MANNING
PARTNERSHIP
251–253 LONDON ROAD EAST,
BATHEASTON, BATH BA1 7RL
TEL. 01225 852 727
FAX 01225 852 852
SALES@MANNINGPARTNERSHIP.
CO.UK

THIS EDITION DISTRIBUTED IN
THE USA BY NATIONAL BOOK
NETWORK
4720 BOSTON WAY
LANHAM, MD 20706
TEL. 301 459 3366
FAX 301 459 1705
WWW.NBNBOOKS.COM

THIS EDITION DISTRIBUTED IN
CANADA BY GENERAL
PUBLISHING
895 DON MILLS ROAD
400–402 PARK CENTRE,
TORONTO, ONTARIO M3C 1W3
TEL. 416 445 3333
FAX 416 445 5991
WWW.GENPUB.COM

THIS EDITION DISTRIBUTED IN AUSTRALIA BY
SANDSTONE PUBLISHING
UNIT 1, 360 NORTON STREET,
LEICHHARDT, NEW SOUTH WALES 2040
TEL. 02 9560 7888; FAX 02 9560 7488;
SALES@SANDSTONEPUBLISHING.COM.AU

THIS EDITION DISTRIBUTED IN NEW ZEALAND
BY THE FIVE MILE PRESS (NZ) LTD
PO BOX 33-1071 TAKAPUNA,
UNIT 11/101-111 DIANA DRIVE
GLENFIELD, AUCKLAND 10
TEL. (09) 444 4144; FAX (09) 444 4518
FIVEMILENZ@CLEAR.NET.NZI

PUBLISHER: JOANNA LORENZ
SENIOR EDITOR: LINDSAY PORTER
PHOTOGRAPHER: PETER WILLIAMS
STYLIST: GEORGINA RHODES
DESIGNERS: PETER BUTLER AND
SUSANNAH GOOD
ILLUSTRATORS: MADELEINE DAVID AND
VANA HAGGERTY
PRODUCTION CONTROLLER: JOANNA KING

PRINTED AND BOUND IN CHINA

ACKNOWLEDGEMENTS
The author and publishers would like to thank the following for supplying the props for photography:
The Holding Company, 243-245 Kings Road, London SW3; Jos Graham Oriental Textiles, 10 Ecclestone Street, London SW1;
Paperchase, 213 Tottenham Court Road, London W1; V.V.Rouleaux, 10 Symons Street, London SW3; Robert Young Antiques, 68 Battersea Bridge Road,
London SW11.

PICTURE CREDITS
Page 8, e t archive; pages 9 (left) and 11 (right), Victoria and Albert Museum; page 9 (bottom), Bridgeman Art Library; pages 10 and 11 (left), Hutchinson
Library

CONTENTS

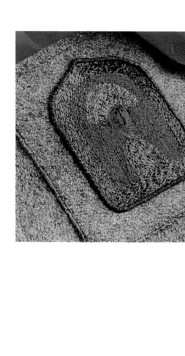

INTRODUCTION

THE VERSATILITY OF MACHINE EMBROIDERY HAS ENABLED CRAFTSPEOPLE AND NEEDLEWORKERS TO EXPERIMENT WITH A WIDE RANGE OF EFFECTS TO PRODUCE TRULY ORIGINAL PIECES. WHETHER YOU ARE DRAWN TO TRADITIONAL APPLIQUÉ AND SHADOW-WORK, OR WISH TO EXPERIMENT WITH MORE UNUSUAL MATERIALS, THE 25 PROJECTS IN THIS BOOK PROVIDE A COMPLETE COLLECTION OF BEAUTIFUL ITEMS TO MAKE. THE GALLERY OF WORK BY CONTEMPORARY DESIGNERS OFFERS FURTHER INSPIRATION FOR EXPLORING THE CRAFT.

Left: Among the many techniques and effects that can be achieved with machine embroidery are shadow-work on the shirt and waistcoat pocket, and appliqué on the cushion.

HISTORY OF MACHINE EMBROIDERY

As would be expected with a craft dependent on technology, machine embroidery is a fairly recent development in the history of textile design and needlework. Embroidered textiles have been in evidence for centuries, in all cultures, and have always been highly prized for their skill and workmanship. Since the advent of the domestic sewing machine, the time and patience required for embroidery has been halved, enabling designers to achieve wonderful results with less of the painstaking labour.

Originally, embroidery was an activity for the upper classes. During the 19th century, upper- and middle-class ladies were kept idle as a mark of their wealth. The only pastimes considered suitable for a lady of rank were those which confirmed her femininity, emphasizing qualities desirable in women: charitable acts showed her compassion, while embroidery demonstrated her delicacy, dexterity and patience. Pattern books of popular motifs such as flowers, hearts and animals were produced especially for this market. Homes were full of the produce of women's leisure hours: tablecloths, cushions and samplers were displayed to demonstrate the maker's patient, self-absorbed nature.

Machine embroidery is the antithesis of these restrictive concepts. It is a craft for people with limited patience whose priority is creativity over occupation. The great appeal of machine embroidery is its speed. Designs can be realized in a matter of hours, while fleeting ideas can be captured. Working with such immediacy is a distinct advantage in the creative process, as new ideas for texture and shape may be born from mistakes and the direction of a piece can be changed at will.

Right: Portrait of Madame Dange Anne Jarry by Louis Tocque (1696–1772). The sitter is depicted making gold knots in lace, illustrating the connection between embroidery and the aristocracy. The labour-intensive, decorative nature of the work ensured it was a luxury for the privileged few.

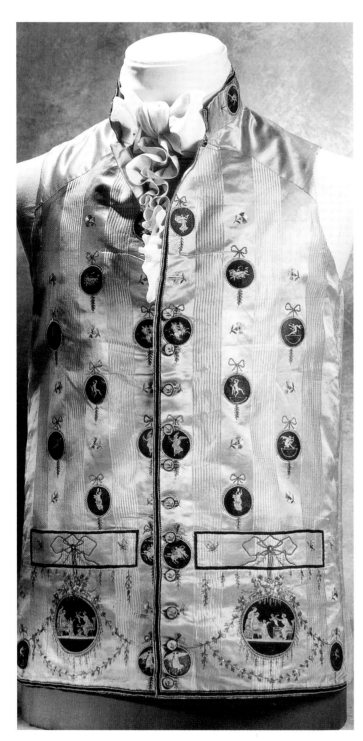

Left: Man's silk waistcoat of the 18th century. The printed motifs on the silk are further embellished with hand-embroidered detail.

Below: Detail of a skirt from Crete. This lavish embroidery was worked in silk, providing a deep border for a skirt for holidays and other special occasions.

Machine embroidery has much to do with the process of drawing and painting. With practice, the embroiderer learns to use the needle with dexterity and fluidity, much as an artist uses a pencil. Stitches can be used to create different textures and densities. Areas of colour are applied by stitchwork or appliquéd fabrics. The texture of the threads and fabrics chosen adds a third dimension to the work.

Embroidery as the art of embellishing existing fabric with threads and other materials has been practised since the times of the ancient Egyptians. Throughout history and in most cultures of the world, men and women have used embroidery to decorate clothing. Until this century, embroidery was a laborious process requiring many hours of skilled labour. Embroidered items were expensive and affordable only to the nobility, the upper classes and the church. Embroidery denoted rank and status and as such was desired and highly prized.

As long ago as the 1790s, manufacturers were toying with the possibilities of producing a sewing machine. During the 19th century, industry developed embroidery machines such as the Cornelly machine for decorative chain stitch, but

these were for factory use only. Domestic machines did not appear on the market until much later in the century. These were fixed-needle machines which could not produce a zigzag – the embroiderer had to move the fabric rapidly from side to side to produce this stitch, a manoeuvre which took great dexterity and skill.

In the 1880s, technicians at the Singer sewing machine company were employed to produce "art" pictures with satin and zigzag stitches on domestic treadle machines. They depicted the popular Victorian images of sentimentalized animals, portraits, landscapes and seascapes or were copies of well-known paintings. With the advent of electric sewing machines, Singer realized the potential for and the interest in domestically produced embroidery. In 1911, they published a book which was called *Singer Instructions for Art Embroidery*. It contained lessons for lace making, appliqué and free embroidery.

Later guides were written by a technician and teacher at Singer, Dorothy Benson, who published *Machine Embroidery: the Artistic Possibilities of the Singer Sewing Machine*, for Singer, and the more popular *Your Machine Embroidery*, for Sylvan Press in 1952. She was a skilled technician and probably the first to see the creative possibilities for embroiderers. As a teacher she influenced and inspired a great many women, one of whom was Rebecca Crompton, an artist and head of women's craft, dress and embroidery at Croydon School of Art. She used hand embroidery in conjunction with the machine, and

experimented with colour and techniques to create texture. Her unconventional approach has left a lasting legacy within the field of machine embroidery.

Today, designers and needleworkers can allow their imagination free-reign, with almost limitless scope for invention, and for exploring the use of new materials. This freedom is the very essence of machine embroidery.

Right: Evening dress in silk organza with machine-embroidered detail by Elsa Schiaparelli, 1953.

Opposite: Embroidered material panels from Goa, with inset shisha mirrors.

Below: Young Rajasthani women. Their garments are embellished with machine-embroidered details and borders.

GALLERY

ONE OF THE JOYS OF MACHINE EMBROIDERY IS ITS SHEER VERSATILITY: IT CAN BE USED AS EXPRESSIVELY AS PAINT OR IT CAN BE USED TO BUILD UP A DESIGN IN THREE DIMENSIONS. THE WORK SHOWN ON THESE PAGES DEMONSTRATES THESE QUALITIES, AND REPRESENTS A CROSS-SECTION OF CONTEMPORARY DESIGNS. EACH OF THE ARTISTS HAS BROUGHT A UNIQUE APPROACH TO EMBROIDERY, AND MAY INSPIRE YOU TO EXPLORE THE POTENTIAL OF THE MEDIUM.

Above: EMBROIDERED BROOCHES
These delightful, stamp-size brooches were embroidered using rayon threads on cotton, linen and silk. The designer has a background in printed textiles, but, drawn by the richness of the effects possible with threads and fabrics, gradually moved to machine embroidery to decorate and embellish her designs.
LINDA MILLER

Right: EMBROIDERED FAN DESIGN
This beautiful piece was created by alternating layers of machine stitching and appliqué on felt to achieve a depth and complexity of design reminiscent of the countryside which inspired it. The fan shape is often used by the designer to enhance the design.
LINDA CHILTON

Left: CUSHION COVER
Hand and machine stitching formed the decoration of this unbleached cotton cushion cover. The designer employs machine embroidery as skilfully as a pen to outline the quirky figures.
MICHELLE HOLMES

Above: SILK EMBROIDERED TOP HATS
These unique hats were both constructed and embellished with machine embroidery. Layers of silk were appliquéd and cut to reveal the fabric underneath on the left-hand hat. The hat on the right was decorated with trapped threads and silk.
JILLI BLACKWOOD

Right: BROOCHES AND EARRINGS
The rich diversity of folk costume throughout the world inspired the design of these jewellery pieces. They were created using a combination of hand and machine stitching, worked on vanishing muslin, which disintegrates upon contact with the heat of an iron. Tiny beads were then hand stitched in place.
JANICE GILMORE

Below: SILK APPLIQUÉ CUSHIONS
The vibrant effect of these cushions was achieved by using a combination of appliqué and decorative zigzag and free stitches, to build up layer upon layer of brilliant colour.
LORNA MOFFAT

Opposite: EMBROIDERED OVERSHIRT
This stunning piece was worked on vanishing muslin. The appliquéd pieces were stitched with two contrasting threads in the needle. The pieces were couched over piping cord.
ISABEL STANLEY

Right: EMBROIDERED
BRASS BROOCHES
Hand-cut and beaten brass
forms the backing of these
richly decorated brooches.
The designer worked the
machine embroidery in
whip stitch on fine fabric,
which was then cut away
and glued to the brass.
JUDY CLAYTON

Left: LINEN SCARF
Cotton fabrics were
machine-appliquéd to a
loose-weave linen scarf to
create this delightful
design. Additional
decorations were screen-
printed on
to the fabric.
RACHEL HOWARD

Above: HEART EARRINGS
AND BROOCH
These pieces were built
up by appliquéing the
basic motifs with metallic
thread on to a strong
background fabric of
calico. The decorative
front was stitched on to
a background of calico
and stuffed. Gold fabric
paint was applied to the
back and edges.
CLARE SOWDEN

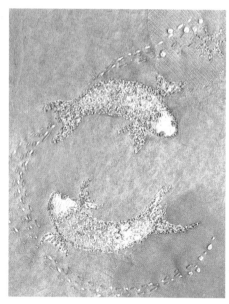

Right: COTTON
CUSHION COVER
Unbleached cotton forms
the background of this
cushion cover, which
was then embellished
with a mixture of
machine-appliquéd
fabrics and screen-
printed designs.
RACHEL HOWARD

Left: EMBROIDERED
BUTTONS
These witty designs appear
to be sketched on to the
buttons, and the designer
has played with the
textures and effects
possible with stitching.
A single line is used in
some places, while others
have been filled in by
stitching over the same
area several times.
MICHELLE HOLMES

Above: PISCES PICTURE
The wonderful depth and
atmosphere of this picture
was achieved by layering
pieces of translucent and
textured fabrics for the
background, and then
machine stitching the main
design with a mixture of
coloured and metallic
threads. Further
decoration was added with
hand stitching.
KAREN HALL

MATERIALS

OST OF THE MATERIALS USED FOR MACHINE EMBROIDERY CAN BE PURCHASED FROM CRAFT SHOPS OR DEPARTMENT STORES. VIRTUALLY ANY FABRIC CAN BE MACHINE EMBROIDERED. CONSIDER HOW THE TEXTURE WILL AFFECT YOUR FINISHED PIECE AND CHOOSE FABRICS ACCORDINGLY. COTTON AND SILK ARE EASY TO HANDLE, AND FELT, PLASTICS AND LEATHER PRODUCE INTERESTING RESULTS. THE MATERIALS LISTED BELOW WILL MAKE SPECIFIC TASKS SIMPLER.

Buttons and beads come in a range of shapes and sizes and a variety of materials, such as plastic, glass, wood and bone.

Cord is usually couched on to fabric or covered in stitchwork.

Fabrics are available in many textures and colours: metallic organza, silk, chiffon, satin and velvet. Cotton ticking will provide a firm base (with grid lines) for many designs

Fusible interlining is used to bond appliqué fabrics to the ground fabric temporarily during stitching. Templates can be marked out on the paper backing.

Hand embroidery threads are available in skeins and can be couched or stitched to enhance machine embroidery.

Invisible thread is a strong transparent thread used to stitch beads on to embroidery. It must be secured firmly.

Machine embroidery threads are available in every imaginable colour and in different strengths. They are more lustrous than sewing threads.

Metallic machine embroidery threads are very popular and are available in many colours as well as shades of gold, bronze and silver. Be careful when stitching at high speeds, as occasionally the thread will snap. Some metallic threads are twisted with matt colours for a less glittery effect.

Self-adhesive felt can be applied to the back of the embroidery.

Sewing threads are used for constructing pieces or when lustrous stitchwork is not desired.

Stabilizers should be used to prevent puckering and distortion of the fabric. Water-soluble polythene will stabilize open-work and sheer fabrics. It pulls away after immersion in cold water, although it can simply be torn away or dabbed with water to remove. It can be used as a template over textured fabrics or to create free-standing embroidery. Hot water-soluble stabilizer can also be used but the embroidery may lose some colour and become stiff. Also available is vanishing muslin, which disintegrates when heated, although scorching may occur and fibres may be difficult to remove. For heavier fabrics use lightweight paper or non-woven interfacing, which can be torn or pulled away after stitching.

Textured threads are available in metallic shades and colours. They can be difficult to use and work best when used in conjunction with a coloured thread in the same needle.

Wool threads are matt, textured threads which work well on woollen fabrics. They can be used in the bobbin or on top of the sewing machine.

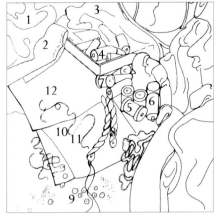

1 metallic organza
2 cotton ticking
3 chiffon
4 machine embroidery threads
5 metallic embroidery threads
6 wool threads
7 sewing thread
8 hand embroidery thread
9 beads
10 cord
11 self adhesive felt
12 water soluble polythene

EQUIPMENT

YOUR MOST IMPORTANT PIECE OF EQUIPMENT IS, OF COURSE, THE SEWING MACHINE. MAKE SURE THE FEED CAN BE LOWERED EASILY, AND THAT THE TOP AND BOBBIN TENSION CAN BE ALTERED. THERE IS NO NEED TO USE A MACHINE WITH A SPECIAL EMBROIDERY PROGRAMME; THE DESIGNS IN THIS BOOK CAN ALL BE ACHIEVED BY VARYING BASIC STITCHES. ADDITIONAL PIECES OF EQUIPMENT MAY BE NEEDED FOR SPECIFIC PROJECTS, AS LISTED BELOW.

Acrylic varnish stiffens embroidery.

Bobbins It is useful to have a number of bobbins to save time unwinding before refilling with another thread.

Dressmaker's carbon is used to transfer designs to fabric.

Dyes for hot and cold water are available and can be mixed to give interesting and unusual shades. Use fabrics with a high percentage of natural fibres for the best results. It is worthwhile to dye a number of fabrics in a variety of colours before creating an appliqué piece. Remember to fix dyes according to the manufacturer's instructions.

Embroidery hoops A wooden hand embroidery hoop can be used for machine embroidery if the inner ring is wrapped with strips of cotton to improve tautness. Specialized machine embroidery hoops with spring closures are more convenient.

Fabric glue can be used in place of fusible interlining to bond fabrics.

Fabric paints are water-based, non-toxic paints that are fixed by ironing.

Fabric pens are used to draw on fabric.

Feet For most embroidery a darning foot should be used, although a presser foot will give a cleaner satin stitch. You can work without a foot, although the thread will tend to snap more frequently.

Gutta is applied using a gutta dispenser to draw a line of even thickness onto fabric. Gutta is available in a variety of colours, metallics and transparent.

Hand-sewing needles Use a selection of needles with larger eyes for hand-stitching with thicker thread. Use a fine beading needle to stitch tiny beads.

Iron Embroidery should be pressed on the wrong side to prevent scorching or flattening the fibres. Set the temperature so as not to damage the least heat-tolerant fabric or thread.

Machine needles Choose a needle that is the right size for the thread. Extra fine and metallic threads require 70/10 or 80/12. Most other threads require 80/12 or 90/14. Heavy, textured and double threads require 100/16 or 110/18.

Masking tape is used to hold fabric taut over templates.

Metal rules are used for drawing straight lines and reducing or enlarging designs.

Pair of compasses are used to make scallop templates and draw circles.

PVA glue can be used to varnish paper embroidery.

Set squares are used for finding a right-angle on a design or fabric.

Sewing machine The machine should have a free arm and a detachable bed for ease of movement. Take care of the machine: clean and oil it regularly to prevent stitch problems.

Scissors Use dressmaker's shears for cutting fabric. Use embroidery scissors for cutting away threads and trimming.

Stencil paper is available in a waxy yellow finish. Cut out stencils with paper scissors or a craft knife.

Tape measures are flexible measuring tools ideal for measuring fabric.

Tissue paper is used as tracing paper. It can also be pinned to the wrong side of the fabric and removed after stitching.

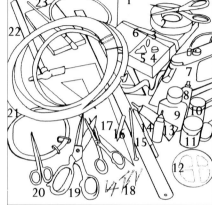

1 sewing machine
2 masking tape
3 tape measure
4 bobbin
5 presser foot
6 darning foot
7 iron
8 fabric pen
9 acrylic varnish
10 fabric paint
11 fabric glue
12 dyes
13 gutta
14 vanishing fabric marker
15 metal rule
16 dressmaker's marker pencil
17 set square
18 dressmaker's pins
19 dressmaker's shears
20 embroidery scissors
21 embroidery hoops
22 hammer
23 palette and paintbrush

Tracing paper is useful for making templates and transferring designs.

Transfers are available in many designs. They are ironed on to the fabric.

Tweezers are useful for removing tissue paper and stabilizer from embroidery and threads from the bobbin case.

Vanishing fabric markers are available in purple and pink and will fade with exposure to air or water. Dressmaker's marker pencils can also be used.

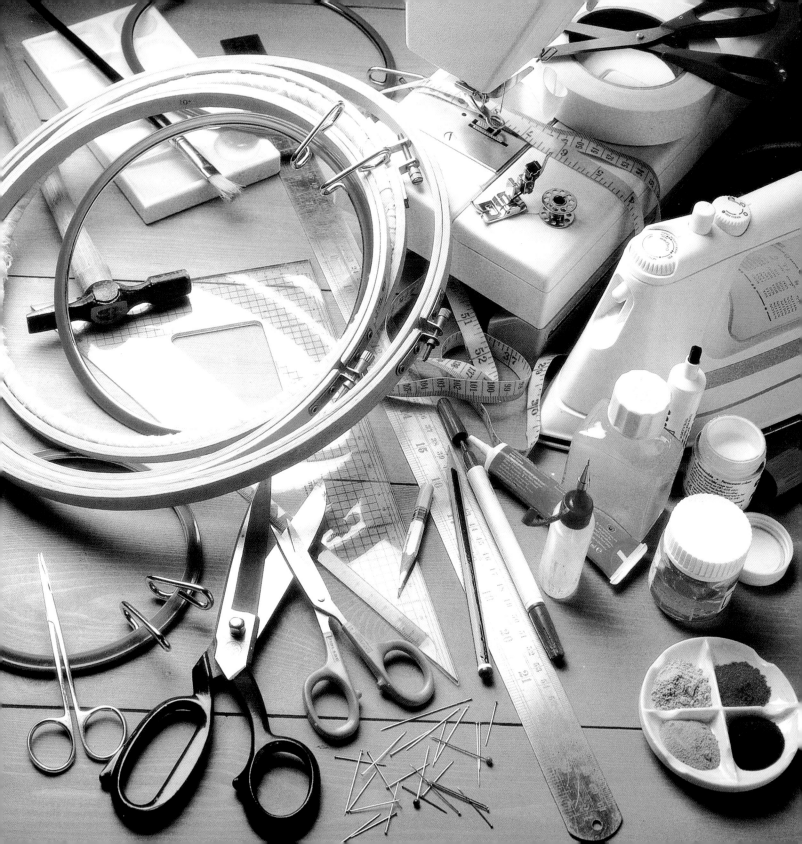

BASIC TECHNIQUES

MANY PEOPLE UNDERSTAND MACHINE EMBROIDERY TO MEAN THE READY-DESIGNED PATTERNS THAT CAN BE ACHIEVED WITH SOME MACHINES, BUT IN FACT, IT REFERS TO THE FREE STITCHING THAT CAN BE ACHIEVED WITH A BASIC SEWING MACHINE. IF YOUR MACHINE IS CAPABLE OF ZIGZAG STITCH, YOU CAN LEARN TO USE IT TO CREATE AN ALMOST INFINITE VARIETY OF EFFECTS. IT IS BEST TO READ THE MANUAL PROVIDED WITH THE MACHINE, TO SEE WHAT IT IS CAPABLE OF DOING. START SLOWLY, TAKING TIME TO PRACTISE WORKING SIMPLE OUTLINES AND OTHER SHAPES, BEFORE PROGRESSING TO MORE ADVANCED TECHNIQUES. DON'T WORRY IF THE NEEDLE BREAKS AS YOU LEARN TO MANIPULATE THE FABRIC — IT HAPPENS TO THE BEST EMBROIDERERS.

PREPARATION

On a domestic sewing machine, the direction and size of the stitch are controlled by the presser foot and the feed, which is the raised part that lies on the bed. Once these factors are removed, any size of stitch in any direction can be made. The feed should therefore be lowered or covered up. Many machines have a darning function which lowers the feed automatically, others should be covered up and the stitch length set to 0. Some embroiderers prefer to work without a presser foot, while others use a darning foot which prevents the fabric from bouncing up and down and the fingers from being stitched.

The fabric being embroidered needs to be stretched in an embroidery hoop. For hand embroidery, the fabric lies over the inner ring. For machine embroidery, place the fabric right side up in the outer ring and press the inner ring inside the outer. The fabric will then lie flat against the machine bed. Stretch the fabric in the hoop taut like a drum, pulling in the direction of the warp and weft. If the hoop is wooden, it will probably not slide under the foot, so sand or file down a small area on the upper side of the rings.

Beginners are advised to practise before starting any project. A test piece should be worked with the machine at a slow speed, if possible. Set the stitch width to 0, lower the presser foot to engage the top tension, work a few stitches to secure the threads and trim the ends to prevent them from becoming entangled in the work. Either hold the hoop and manoeuvre it gently, or place your fingers firmly either side of the foot and guide the fabric. Do not jerk the fabric but keep it moving steadily. Practise stitching in every direction, working spirals and filling stitches and practising drawing and writing.

For regular stitching, set the tension so that the bottom thread cannot be seen on the right side and the top thread cannot be seen on the wrong side. Interesting effects can be achieved when the tension is altered. By loosening the bobbin tension, the top thread will lie across the surface as if couched. If the top tension is tightened, the loops of the bottom thread will pull through to the right side. Different textures and weights of fabric will also have an effect on the appearance of the stitching. Adjust according to the manufacturer's instructions. A small screwdriver is required to alter the tension on the bobbin.

STITCH PROBLEMS

To prevent problems during stitching, remove lint and threads from the bobbin case regularly. Oil the machine according to the manufacturer's instructions.

If the threads break, the needle breaks or stitches are not properly formed, check that: the needle is the correct type for the machine; the needle is correctly fitted; the needle is not blunt or bent and is the correct size for the thread; the sewing machine is correctly threaded.

If the needle breaks, check that: the top tension is not too tight; the fabric is not being moved too forcibly and causing the needle to strike the needle plate or bobbin case.

If the top thread breaks, check that: the top tension is not too tight; the top thread is not knotted; the presser bar is lowered. Also, try working the first few stitches slowly.

If the bobbin thread breaks, check that: the bobbin tension is not too tight; the thread is not unevenly wound; there are no trapped threads caught in the bobbin case.

If stitches are missed, check that: the needle is suitable for both the thread and fabric; the fabric is lying flat against the needle plate.

If the fabric is puckering, check that: the top and bobbin tensions are not too tight; the fabric has not been removed forcibly from the machine; the stitches are not too long; the thread is not too thick for the fabric (if it is, use a stabilizer). The timing can be checked by lowering the needle and drawing up a thread (use a regular size of needle and thread). If the thread is not drawing up properly or the needle is striking any part of the bobbin, the timing may be out. This is a mechanical problem which requires a specialist's attention. If there are none in your area, contact the manufacturer.

TRANSFERRING ORIGINAL DESIGNS

Scaling up templates
Trace the template on to tissue paper and lay it over a piece of graph paper. Using an appropriate scale, enlarge the template on to a second piece of graph paper, copying the shape from each smaller square to each larger one.

Using fabric markers
Draw around the template with a water-soluble fabric marker or dressmaker's marking pencil.

Using dressmaker's carbon paper
Lay the carbon paper face down on the right side of the fabric and lay the traced design on top. Draw over the lines with a ballpoint pen.

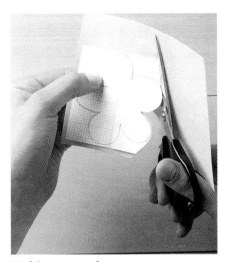

Making a template
Lay the sketch on to thin card and cut around the outline using paper scissors.

Using a light box or window
Tape the design to a light box or window and then tape the fabric over it. Trace over the design with a fabric marker.

Using tailor's chalk
If you are using a dark fabric, mark out the design with tailor's chalk. It will leave a fairly powdery texture that is easy to brush off. ▶

Using water-soluble polythene

If a design cannot be drawn on to a textured fabric with a fabric marker, trace the design on to a piece of water-soluble polythene and pin it to the right side of the fabric. Dissolve after stitching.

Non-woven stabilizer

A non-woven interfacing or lightweight paper should be pinned to the wrong side of the fabric for heavy embroidery or on lightweight fabric, to add body and prevent the fabric from distorting.

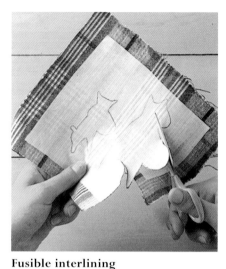

Fusible interlining

1 Fusible interlining is useful for stabilizing appliqué pieces, as it binds on to the fabric with an iron. You can then cut round the shape to be appliquéd, with the interlining in place to act as a stiffener.

Using tissue paper

Trace the design on to a piece of tissue paper and pin it to the wrong side of the fabric. Remove after stitching.

Water-soluble stabilizer

Use water-soluble polythene to support lightweight fabric, lace or open-work.

2 Fusible interlining has a backing paper that can be peeled off. The pieces can then be pressed in place on the ground fabric.

SIMPLE APPLIQUÉ

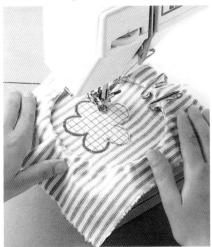

Embroidered appliqué pieces
Draw the shape on the fabric with a fabric marker and embroider the pattern over the edges of the outline.

Straight stitch appliqué
1 Cut out the shape, leaving 1 cm (½ in) allowance all around. Press the allowance to the wrong side, snipping away corners and curves.

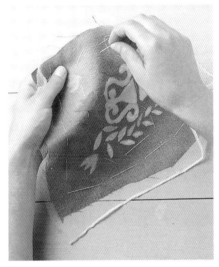

Shadow appliqué
1 Work the appliqué pieces using one of the methods described previously, then pin and tack a piece of sheer fabric over the design.

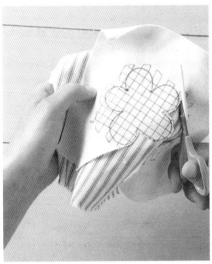

Zigzag or satin stitch appliqué
Pin the appliqué piece to the ground fabric and stitch around the outline. Trim away the excess fabric close to the stitched line. Work a zigzag stitch around the outline, covering raw edges. This can be followed by a second line of satin stitch.

2 Pin the piece to the fabric and work a straight stitch all round.

2 Use matching sewing thread to stitch over the sheer fabric, close to the stitches on the appliquéd pieces.

STITCHES

To prepare the sewing machine for machine embroidery, lower the feed and attach a darning foot.

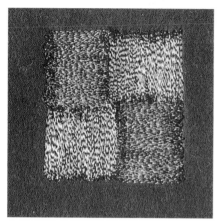

Whip stitch

This produces a beaded effect as the lower thread is brought through to the surface. It is particularly effective when the bobbin thread is of a contrasting colour. Loosen the bobbin tension and tighten the top tension for this stitch.

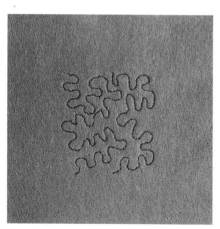

Vermicelli stitch

This is a filling stitch particularly effective for quilting, or for cable stitching with gold thread.

Cable stitch or mock couching

The thread appears to be couched in place. This is a method for embroidering heavy threads which cannot pass through the eye of a needle. The heavier thread is wound on to a bobbin and the bobbin tension is loosened so that the thread can pass through easily. Tighten the top tension. Work the piece from the wrong side. Alternatively, loosen the bobbin tension so that the bobbin thread forms into loops.

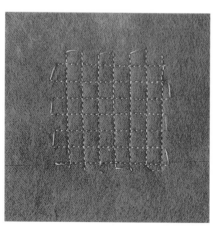

Cross-hatching

This is used to fill areas with colour or texture. Set the sewing machine for regular stitching and attach the presser foot. Using the foot as a guide, stitch out the grid.

Satin stitch

This can be worked in free machine embroidery or set for regular stitching. Set the stitch width as desired. Move the embroidery hoop slowly so that the stitches lie next to each other. The width of the stitch can be varied along the line by altering the dial, although this requires a certain degree of skill. The stitches at the corners are tapered to a point.

Looped stitch

Work whip stitch, tightening the top tension and loosening the bottom. Remove the top thread with a needle. Bond a piece of fusible interlining to the wrong side.

Zigzag filler
Set the stitch width as desired. Move the fabric from side to side. The area can be filled at a 45-degree angle. To add shading, work several rows of stitching, making the edges jagged so that subsequent layers will blend into the previous ones.

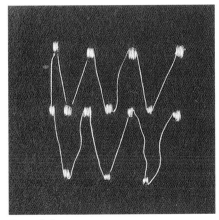

French knots
Set the stitch width to the size of the knot desired. Work a solid satin stitch over one spot several times. Do not cut the threads between dots. The dots can be cut with a stitch ripper to create tufts to secure the threads. Bond a piece of fusible interlining to the wrong side.

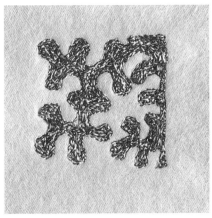

Double threads
These can be used to produce a subtle two-toned effect or to tone down the impact of a metallic thread. Two threads are threaded through the needle. Use a larger-sized needle and a looser top tension. Using a second thread can help the passage of a weak or textured thread through the tension wheels.

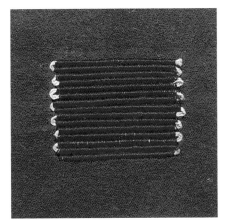

Couching
The fabric should be backed with a stabilizer for couching. Draw the outline of the design and lay a piece of thick thread or piping along the line. Set the stitch width to the width of the piping or thread and then stitch a satin stitch or a zigzag stitch along its length.

Couched yarn with straight stitch
Lay a yarn around the outline and work a straight stitch along the centre of the yarn.

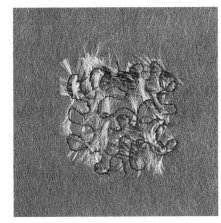

Trapped threads
Cut small pieces of thread and lay them on the fabric. Work a vermicelli stitch over the threads.

APPLIQUÉD NAPKINS

CARTOON ANIMALS BALANCE GLASSES OF RED WINE ON THEIR SILVER TRAYS. CHOOSE CONTRASTING CHECKED FABRICS, GINGHAMS OR FLOWERED FABRICS TO CO-ORDINATE WITH YOUR TABLE LINEN. APPLIQUÉ PIECES ARE BONDED TO THE GROUND FABRIC BEFORE STITCHING. THE FUSIBLE INTERLINING AVAILABLE NOW IS MORE CONVENIENT AND EFFECTIVE THAN THE PASTES AND STARCHES OF THE PAST. INTERLINING HAS A DUAL PURPOSE: NOT ONLY DOES IT BOND FABRICS TO GIVE A SMOOTH, CRISP FINISH, BUT IT ALSO LINES THE UPPER FABRIC, PREVENTING DARK OR PATTERNED GROUND FABRIC FROM SHOWING THROUGH. MOST INTER-LININGS HAVE A PAPER BACKING ON WHICH THE DESIGN CAN BE TRACED. ONCE THE INTERLINING IS BONDED TO THE UPPER FABRIC, THE SHAPE CAN BE CUT OUT.

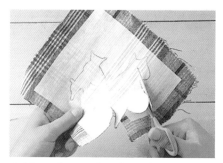

1 Trace the template from the back of the book, enlarging as required. Trace the outlines on to the backing of the interlining. Press the interlining to bond it to the wrong side of the contrasting fabric. Cut out the shapes.

2 Remove the backing and press the pieces in place on the napkin. Draw on the details as a guide.

3 Lower the feed on the sewing machine and attach a darning foot. Place the napkin in an embroidery hoop. Stitch around the shapes, close to the edge, in a contrasting colour. Stitch the arms and the chin of the cat.

4 Using metallic thread, work each tray in a spiral from the centre to the outline. Stitch the facial features, the bow ties and the glasses in contrasting colours.

5 Pull away the warp and weft threads from the edges of the napkin, using a needle to separate them. Raise the feed on the sewing machine and attach a presser foot. Choose an appropriate stitch length and a medium zigzag width. Stitch around the napkin to secure the fringed edges.

MATERIALS AND EQUIPMENT YOU WILL NEED

FUSIBLE INTERLINING • CONTRASTING PATTERNED FABRIC • IRON • EMBROIDERY SCISSORS •
CHECKED FABRIC, 40 x 40 CM (16 x 16 IN) FOR EACH NAPKIN • PEN • DARNING FOOT • NEEDLE SIZE 90/14 •
EMBROIDERY HOOP • COLOURED AND METALLIC MACHINE EMBROIDERY THREADS • NEEDLE • PRESSER FOOT

ORANGE TREE PICTURE

THIS CHARMING COUNTRY-COTTAGE STYLE FRAMED PICTURE DEPICTS AN ORANGE TREE, WITH LEAVES PICKED OUT IN GREENS AND YELLOWS, ON A FABRIC BACKGROUND. THE DESIGNER, LUCINDA GANDERTON, HAS CHOSEN TICKING AS THE GROUND FABRIC BUT GINGHAM AND CHECKED FABRIC MAKE ATTRACTIVE ALTERNATIVES. THE MOTIFS OF THE DESIGN COULD BE ECHOED THROUGHOUT A ROOM, STITCHED ON TO A TABLECLOTH OR IN THE CENTRE OF A CUSHION, FOR EXAMPLE. THIS DESIGN MAKES A GOOD FIRST PROJECT AS THE EMBROIDERY IS WORKED IN STRAIGHT AND ZIGZAG STITCHES.

1 On tracing paper draw the design to the size required. Lay a piece of dressmaker's carbon paper face down between the tracing paper and the fabric, matching the trunk to the grain of the fabric. Draw around the lines of the design in ballpoint pen, pressing firmly.

2 Lower the feed on the sewing machine and attach a darning foot. Place the fabric in an embroidery hoop. Work the oranges in straight stitch in a spiral from the centre to the outline.

3 Work the leaves in various shades of green, stitching back and forth to fill the shapes.

4 Work the trunk in straight stitch, then set a medium zigzag width and fill in the ornamental urn shape

5 Iron the piece on the wrong side. Cut a piece of card slightly smaller than the inner section of the frame. Trim the fabric to the size of the card, leaving a 2.5 cm (1 in) allowance all around. Lay the card on the wrong side of the fabric. Using a needle and thread, stretch the sides of the fabric over the card and work long stitches between opposite edges. Stitch the top and bottom edges in the same way. Stitch the folded corners neatly in place. Place the piece in the frame and secure it in place with masking tape.

MATERIALS AND EQUIPMENT YOU WILL NEED

TRACING PAPER • BALLPOINT PEN • DRESSMAKER'S CARBON PAPER • TICKING FABRIC, 40 x 40 CM (16 x 16 IN) •
DARNING FOOT • NEEDLE SIZE 90/14 • EMBROIDERY HOOP • COLOURED MACHINE EMBROIDERY THREADS • IRON • CARD •
EMBROIDERY SCISSORS • NEEDLE • SEWING THREAD • PICTURE FRAME • MASKING TAPE

LINEN WAISTCOAT

APPLIQUÉ AND EMBROIDERY EMBELLISH MANY HAUTE COUTURE GARMENTS AND ADD GREATLY TO THEIR COST BECAUSE OF THE TIME REQUIRED TO PRODUCE SUCH WORK. WITH A LITTLE IMAGINATION, A DRESSMAKER CAN USE UP REMNANTS OF FABRIC TO ADD A LUXURIOUS DECORATION TO ANY GARMENT. THIS WAISTCOAT, DESIGNED BY LOUISE BROWNLOW, DEMONSTRATES THAT BY EMBROIDERING A PARTICULAR AREA, SUCH AS A COLLAR, CUFF OR POCKET, A UNIQUE PIECE IS CREATED. LOUISE USES TRADITIONAL SHADOW AND MULTI-COLOURED APPLIQUÉ. SHEER FABRIC OVERLAYS THE MULTICOLOURED APPLIQUÉ TECHNIQUES ON THE GROUND FABRIC AND THE COLOURS OF THE DESIGN ARE ECHOED IN THE SUBSEQUENT STITCHWORK.

1 Trace the templates from the back of the book, enlarging as required. Trace the design on to a piece of interfacing cut to the size of the pocket pattern piece. Cut out the pocket piece from the fabric, leaving a 2 cm (¾ in) allowance. Lay the interfacing on the wrong side of the pocket piece and press in place. Flip the design for the other pocket and repeat.

2 Cut a piece of silk slightly larger than the urn. Pin and tack to the right side of the pocket.

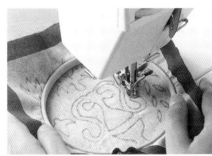

3 Lower the feed on the sewing machine and attach a darning foot. Place the piece in an embroidery hoop, wrong side up. Stitch the outline of the urn shape.

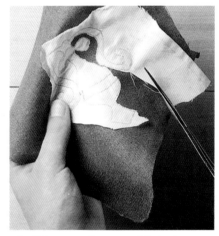

4 Trim away the excess fabric close to the stitched line using sharp embroidery scissors. ▶

MATERIALS AND EQUIPMENT YOU WILL NEED

COMMERCIAL WAISTCOAT PATTERN, MADE UP • MEDIUMWEIGHT INTERFACING, 40 x 40 CM (16 x 16 IN) • LINEN FABRIC TO MATCH WAISTCOAT, 1.5 M x 90 CM (1½ YD x 36 IN) • DRESSMAKER'S SHEARS • IRON • SMALL PIECES OF COLOURED SILK FABRIC • PINS • NEEDLE • TACKING THREAD • DARNING FOOT • NEEDLE SIZE 90/12 • EMBROIDERY HOOP • MATCHING MACHINE EMBROIDERY THREADS • EMBROIDERY SCISSORS • SHEER FABRIC, 40 x 40 CM (16 x 16 IN) • LINING FABRIC, 1.5 M x 90 CM (1½ YD x 36 IN) • PRESSER FOOT • RIBBONS AND MATCHING THREAD

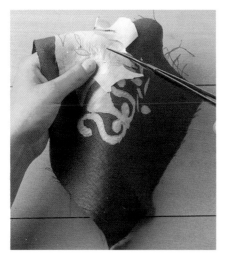

5 aCut a piece of contrasting silk slightly larger than the area of the leaf shapes. Pin and tack it to the right side of the pocket piece and, on the wrong side, stitch the leaf outlines in matching thread. Trim away the fabric close to the stitched line using sharp scissors. Appliqué pink and red flowers to the pocket piece in the same way.

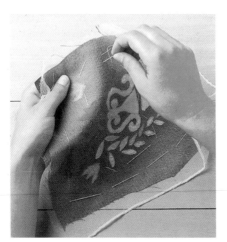

6 On the right side, pin and tack a piece of sheer fabric over the appliquéd design. Cut a pocket facing to the width of the pocket, plus 2 cm (³/₄ in).

7 Using matching thread, stitch the stems and details on the leaves, flowers and urn and around all the outlines. Trim away the excess sheer fabric close to the stitched lines. Work two or three lines of stitching to cover the raw edges.

8 Cut a piece of lining fabric to the size of the pocket pattern piece. Raise the feed on the sewing machine and attach a presser foot. Choose an appropriate stitch length. With right sides facing, stitch the pocket and facing together along the seam. With right sides together, stitch the lining to the pocket piece.

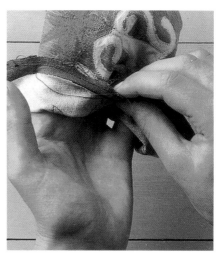

9 Turn the pocket the right way out. Slip stitch the fourth side closed by hand.

10 Trim the top edge of the pocket with two ribbons, using matching sewing thread. Pin and tack the pocket on to the front of the waistcoat. Stitch the pocket in place.

SHADOW APPLIQUÉ SHIRT

DELICATE WOODLAND FLOWERS ARE EMBROIDERED ON THIS GAUZY SHIRT USING SHADOW APPLIQUÉ. TRADITIONALLY, OPAQUE SHAPES ARE APPLIQUÉD TO A GROUND FABRIC BEFORE BEING COVERED BY A SHEER FABRIC, WHICH SOFTENS THE COLOUR AND OUTLINE OF THE APPLIQUÉD SHAPES. THE SHEER FABRIC IS SEWN ON TO EACH SHAPE AND THE EXCESS TRIMMED AWAY. HERE, THE DARKER FABRIC IS APPLIED DIRECTLY TO THE WRONG SIDE OF THE SHEER FABRIC, WHICH FORMS THE GROUND. THE CONTRAST BETWEEN THE DARK AND THE LIGHT FABRIC IS LESSENED WHEN THE LIGHTER COLOUR IS UPPERMOST. A COMMERCIAL SHIRT OR BLOUSE PATTERN WILL DETERMINE THE AMOUNT OF FABRIC REQUIRED. THE BORDER AND FILLING DESIGNS CAN BE ADAPTED TO FIT MOST PATTERN PIECES.

1 Trace the flower templates from the back of the book, enlarging as required. On the shirt pattern pieces, roughly mark the areas to be embroidered (the border and the collar) with a pencil, taking care to avoid the seam and hem allowance. Lay the pattern pieces over the templates and draw the position of each motif, spacing them evenly.

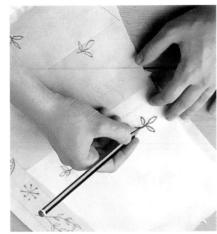

2 Trace the sprig templates from the back of the book, enlarging as required. Cut a piece of paper 20 x 20 cm (8 x 8 in). Draw a small sprig in each corner and one in the centre. Mark the position of the sprigs on the pattern pieces, inside the border design. Lay the paper pattern pieces on the sheer fabric and mark around them with a fabric marker. Cut out the pieces, leaving a 2 cm ($^3/_4$ in) allowance. Lay the fabric over the paper pattern and trace the motifs with a fabric marker.

3 Cut small pieces of coloured fabric slightly larger than the motifs. Pin the coloured pieces to the wrong side of the ground fabric behind the leaf motifs.

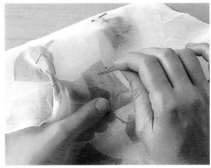

4 Tack the coloured fabric pieces in place around the edges. ▶

aMATERIALS AND EQUIPMENT YOU WILL NEED
COMMERCIAL SHIRT OR BLOUSE PATTERN • PENCIL • PAPER • SHEER FABRIC • FABRIC MARKER • DRESSMAKER'S SHEARS •
SHEER AND SOLID FABRIC, 25 x 90 CM (10 x 36 IN) • PINS • NEEDLE • TACKING THREAD • DARNING FOOT • NEEDLE SIZE 80/12 • EMBROIDERY
HOOP • MATCHING MACHINE EMBROIDERY THREAD • EMBROIDERY SCISSORS • PRESSER FOOT • MATCHING SEWING THREAD

5 Lower the feed on the sewing
machine and attach a darning foot.
Place the fabric in an embroidery hoop
and, using matching thread, work a single
line around each leaf motif.

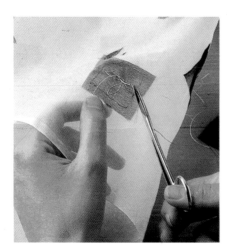

6 On the wrong side, trim away the
tacking threads and the excess
coloured fabric from the stitched line.

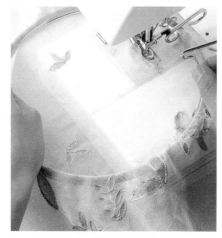

7 Replace the fabric in the hoop and
machine stitch an additional two or
three lines around the leaf shapes to cover
the raw edges. Cut small pieces of the
ground fabric slightly larger than the
envelope shapes and appliqué as described
from step three.

8 Machine stitch the stems two or three
lines thick and fill in the leaf shapes
over the appliquéd pieces. Raise the feed
on the sewing machine and attach a
presser foot. Make up the shirt following
the manufacturer's instructions, using
French seams to enclose raw edges.

PAPER PORTFOLIO

VARIOUS WEIGHTS AND TEXTURES OF HANDMADE AND MANUFACTURED PAPERS MAKE UP THIS SIMPLE APPLIQUÉD COLLAGE. AS WITH FABRICS, THERE ARE AN INFINITE NUMBER OF PAPERS TO CHOOSE FROM. HANDMADE PAPERS ARE THE MOST INTERESTING TO WORK WITH AS THEIR SURFACE IS GENERALLY RAISED AND IRREGULAR. PAPER CAN BE CUT OR TORN, PAINTED OR PRINTED. INTERESTING TEXTURES ARE CREATED WHEN THE PAPER IS FED THROUGH AN UNTHREADED SEWING MACHINE — THE PUNCHED HOLES MAKE A RAISED DOT OR BEAD PATTERN. THE FINISHED COLLAGE IS PAINTED WITH A LAYER OF GLUE WHICH ACTS AS A VARNISH. ALTHOUGH A SEWING MACHINE WILL SEW PAPER EASILY, THE NEEDLE WILL BE BLUNTED AND SHOULD BE CHANGED BEFORE BEGINNING ANOTHER PROJECT.

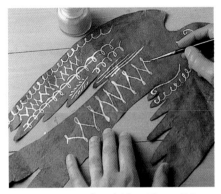

1 Cut a piece of card 40 x 65 cm (16 x 26 in). Using a craft knife and a metal rule, score two lines 30 cm (12 in) from each short edge to make a 5 cm (2 in) spine to the folder. Trace the templates from the back of the book, enlarging as required. Tape the templates and papers to a window or light box and trace the outlines and pattern details. Cut out the swirl designs from one piece of paper with paper scissors. Paint the pattern details of the bird in metallic paint.

2 Glue the background paper with cut-out swirls to the card. Lower the feed on the sewing machine and attach a darning foot. Stitch around the edges of the swirls in a matching thread.

3 Glue the bird shape in place. Set a medium zigzag width and fill the bobbin and the top with contrasting threads for a whip stitch. Work a zigzag stitch around the bird shape.

4 Raise the feed on the sewing machine and attach a presser foot. Set a wide stitch width and fill the bobbin and the top with contrasting threads for a whip stitch. Work a zigzag stitch along the two side edges of the folder. Fold the card along the scored lines and stitch along the top and bottom edges. To varnish the folder, paint it all over with PVA glue and allow to dry. To hold papers inside the folder, draw around a coin to make two card circles. Cut out the circles and punch a small hole in the centre of each. Punch a hole 2.5 cm (1 in) from the edge, in the middle of both side edges. Thread the paper fasteners through the holes in the circles and the folder. Open out the wings on the inside of the folder and attach a piece of string between the two fasteners.

MATERIALS AND EQUIPMENT YOU WILL NEED

CARD • CRAFT KNIFE • METAL RULE • PAPERS • MASKING TAPE • PAPER SCISSORS • METALLIC ACRYLIC PAINT • PAINTBRUSH • PVA GLUE • DARNING FOOT • NEEDLE SIZE 90/14 • MACHINE EMBROIDERY THREADS • PRESSER FOOT • COIN • HOLE PUNCH • TWO PAPER FASTENERS • STRING

BLAZER BADGE

THIS EXOTIC CHARACTER WITH HIS ELABORATE HEADDRESS IS EMBROIDERED IN RICHLY CONTRASTING THREADS ON A BACKGROUND OF INTERFACING. DESIGNED BY SARAH RUBIE, THE BADGE CAN BE STITCHED ON TO A BLAZER OR BLANKET. THIS IS AN IDEAL FIRST PROJECT FOR THE BEGINNER TO PRACTISE FILLING STITCHWORK. THE BACKGROUND FABRIC IS PAINTED SO THAT THE BRIGHT WHITE INTERFACING DOES NOT SHOW THROUGH THE STITCHING.

1 Follow the finished photographs to draw the design, enlarging as required. Make a template from thin card. Lay this on the interfacing and draw around the shapes with a fabric marker or pen.

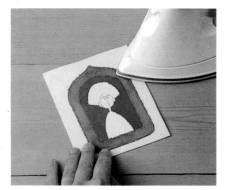

2 Using fabric dyes, paint the background design in areas of solid colour, so that the white interfacing does not show through the stitching. Press with a medium-hot iron to fix the dyes.

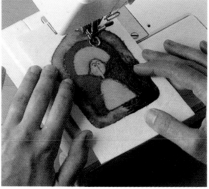

3 Lower the feed on the sewing machine and attach a darning foot. Fill in the design areas in the desired colours by working a straight stitch back and forth.

4 Work the face in a spiral from the centre point to the outline. To give a raised effect, push the dome out from the wrong side.

5 Thread a needle with a dark thread and sew the eyes and nose details. Use gold thread for the stars and the headdress details. Cut out the badge shape close to the outline. Set a medium stitch width and work a satin stitch all round the edge.

MATERIALS AND EQUIPMENT YOU WILL NEED

THIN CARD • NON-WOVEN HEAVYWEIGHT INTERFACING, 20 x 20 CM (8 x 8 IN) • FABRIC MARKER OR PEN • FABRIC DYES • PAINTBRUSH • IRON • DARNING FOOT • NEEDLE SIZE 80/12–90/14 • COLOURED AND METALLIC MACHINE EMBROIDERY THREADS • NEEDLE • EMBROIDERY SCISSORS

KIMONO

THE KIMONO HAS LONG BEEN AN IDEAL CANVAS FOR CREATIVE TEXTILE DESIGN. THE SIMPLE SHAPE LENDS ITSELF TO THE APPLICATION OF A STRIKING PATTERN. THIS PIECE IS EMBROIDERED IN FLOSS THREAD, WHICH IS A LUSTROUS RAYON THREAD USUALLY HAND-STITCHED AS IT IS WEAK. TO COMPENSATE, THE THREAD SHOULD BE WOUND ON THE BOBBIN AND THE TENSION ADJUSTED ACCORDINGLY. THE EMBROIDERY IS WORKED FROM THE WRONG SIDE SO THAT THE FLOSS THREAD WILL LIE FLAT ON THE RIGHT SIDE AND APPEAR TO BE COUCHED DOWN. THIS IS KNOWN AS CABLE STITCH. THE MOTIF SHOULD BE ENLARGED TO THREE DIFFERENT SIZES AND ARRANGED RANDOMLY ON THE CROSS. THE APPLIQUÉ MATCHES THE LINING FABRIC, THUS CO-ORDINATING THE WHOLE GARMENT.

1 Trace the heart and butterfly templates from the back of the book, enlarging them to three different sizes. Trace the outline of a number of motifs on to the paper backing of the fusible interlining. Cut 0.5 m (¹/₂ yd) of lining fabric. Press the interlining to bond it to the wrong side of the lining fabric. Cut out the shapes with embroidery scissors. With dressmaker's shears, cut out the kimono pattern pieces in satin fabric, leaving an allowance of 2.5 cm (1 in) all around. Decide on the positioning of the embroidery. Remove the paper backing from the appliqué pieces and arrange them on the satin fabric. Press the appliqué pieces to bond them into place.

2 Lower the feed on the sewing machine and attach a darning foot. Set a medium zigzag width. Fill the bobbin with a contrasting thread and use a matching thread on top for a whip stitch. Work a zigzag stitch around the appliqué shapes.

3 Cut pieces of tissue paper slightly larger than the design pieces. Trace

the outline and the pattern details of the template for each appliquéd shape. On the wrong side of the satin fabric, carefully match up the tissue paper templates to the appliquéd pieces, using the stitching as a guide. Pin in place.

4 Place the section to be embroidered first in an embroidery hoop. Set the stitch width to 0 and fill the bobbin with contrasting floss thread and the top with matching thread. Cable stitch the pattern two or three lines thick. To stitch the outline, antennae and eyes, fill the bobbin with dark floss thread. Tear away the tissue paper from the wrong side of the embroidery before constructing the kimono using a presser foot.

MATERIALS AND EQUIPMENT YOU WILL NEED

FUSIBLE INTERLINING, 0.5 M (¹/₂ YD) • CONTRASTING LINING FABRIC, 4.5 M X 90 CM (4¹/₂ YD X 36 IN) • DRESSMAKER'S SHEARS • IRON • EMBROIDERY SCISSORS • COMMERCIAL KIMONO PATTERN • SATIN FABRIC, 4 M X 90 CM (4 YD X 36 IN) • DARNING FOOT • NEEDLE SIZE 90/14 • EMBROIDERY HOOP • COLOURED MACHINE EMBROIDERY THREADS • TISSUE PAPER • PINS • COLOURED FLOSS EMBROIDERY THREADS • PRESSER FOOT

PATCHWORK-STYLE CUSHION

SCRAPS OF PATTERNED FABRICS HAVE BEEN CHOSEN TO CONTRAST WITH THE SLUBBED NATURAL LINEN FABRIC TO MAKE AN ATTRACTIVE CUSHION COVER. DESIGNED BY SARAH KING, THE COVER CAN BE APPLIQUÉD WITH FABRICS THAT CO-ORDINATE WITH YOUR OWN FURNISHINGS. TO COMPLEMENT THE MATT FINISH OF THE LINEN FABRIC, COTTON SEWING THREADS WITH A MATT FINISH HAVE BEEN USED. THE ABSTRACT DESIGN IS EMBELLISHED WITH MACHINE EMBROIDERED WHIP STITCH WORKED TO RESEMBLE HAND STITCHING. THE "HAND STITCHES" ARE WORKED EITHER SIDE OF THE ZIP CLOSURE FOR THE FINISHING TOUCH.

1 Cut strips of silk and patterned cotton fabrics and fusible interlining 10 x 30 cm (4 x 12 in). Iron the fusible interlining to bond it to the wrong side of the appliqué fabrics. Mark strips 3 cm (1¼ in) wide across the length of the backed fabrics and cut along the lines. For the topside, cut a piece of linen to the size of the cushion pad, leaving a 2 cm (¾ in) allowance all around, plus an extra 2 cm (¾ in) zip allowance on one long edge. On the topside mark two squares with a marking pencil, the outer the size of the pad and the inner 2 cm (¾ in) smaller. Draw a grid of nine squares inside the smaller square. Peel away the paper backing from the appliqué pieces and position four or five within each square. Press with a medium-hot iron to bond into place.

2 Lower the feed on the sewing machine and attach a darning foot. Place the piece to be embroidered first in an embroidery hoop. Set a medium zigzag width. Fill the bobbin with a light-coloured thread. On top, use a thread which matches the linen for a whip stitch. Work a zigzag stitch all around each appliqué piece.

3 Mark the "hand stitches" in marking pencil between and over all the appliqué pieces.

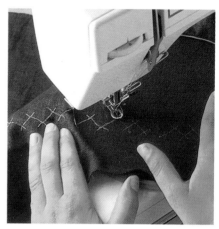

4 Set the stitch width to 0 and work the "hand stitches" in whip stitch, with the dark thread in the bobbin and the lighter thread on top. On both underside pieces, press down the 2 cm (¾ in) zip allowance. Mark a row of "hand stitches" in marking pencil close to the fold and stitch in whip stitch. Insert the zip. Raise the feed on the sewing machine and attach a presser foot. With the wrong sides facing, stitch a straight seam all around the cushion cover, leaving the zip undone. Turn the cover the right way out and stuff with the cushion pad.

MATERIALS AND EQUIPMENT YOU WILL NEED
SILK AND PATTERNED COTTON FABRICS • FUSIBLE INTERLINING • EMBROIDERY SCISSORS • IRON •
LINEN FABRIC, APPROXIMATELY 1.5 M X 90 CM (1½ YD X 36 IN) • DRESSMAKER'S SHEARS • CUSHION PAD • MARKING PENCIL • DARNING FOOT •
NEEDLE SIZE 90/14 • EMBROIDERY HOOP • MATT MACHINE EMBROIDERY THREADS • ZIP • PRESSER FOOT

CHILD'S BLANKET

Influenced by Mexican folk art traditions, these brightly coloured appliqué birds strut across the sober-coloured blanket. Finished with a blanket stitch and decorative buttonhole details, this design will appeal to adults as well as children. The felt patches are appliquéd using a machine satin stitch and sewn all around the pieces are fake hand stitches. Felt squares dyed in a riot of colours are available in department stores and haberdashery shops and are a convenient size. A length of woollen fabric can be purchased or an old blanket embellished. Use a sharp needle and a fine thread to work the satin stitch and check the tension before stitching. Always use a stabilizer when satin stitching.

1 Trace the templates from the back of the book, enlarging as required, and make templates on thin card. Draw round the templates on the felt using a marker. Draw in the details freehand.

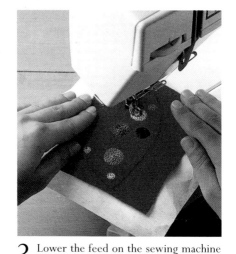

3 Lower the feed on the sewing machine and attach a darning foot. Cut a piece of interfacing and pin it to the wrong side of a second piece of felt. Place this on top of the felt piece with the fusible interlining. Fill in the pattern details with solid stitchwork. For the dots, work a spiral from the centre coming outwards to the outline.

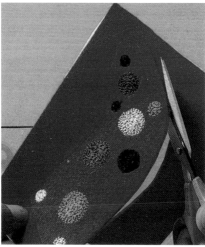

4 Cut out the shapes with sharp embroidery scissors.

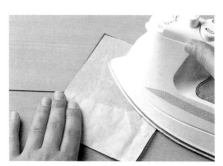

2 Cut a piece of fusible interlining to the size of each felt piece. Press to bond to the wrong side of the felt.

MATERIALS AND EQUIPMENT YOU WILL NEED

Thin card • Small pieces of felt • Fabric marker • Fusible interlining • Dressmaker's shears • Iron • Darning foot • Mediumweight non-woven interfacing • Pins • Needle size 90/14 • Coloured machine embroidery threads • Embroidery scissors • Woollen fabric, 1 x 1.5 m (1 x 1½ yd) • Presser foot • Marker pencil • Embroidery hoop • Needle • Buttons • Metal rule • Hand embroidery thread

5 Remove the paper backing from the fusible interlining. Arrange the shapes on the woollen ground fabric 25 cm (10 in) from the raw edge. Pin in place.

6 Press with a hot iron on the wrong side of the ground fabric to bond the shapes in place.

7 Raise the feed on the sewing machine and attach a presser foot. Cut and pin a piece of interfacing to the wrong side of the ground fabric. Set a medium stitch width and work a satin stitch around each appliqué piece in contrasting thread.

8 At intervals around each piece, satin stitch fake "hand stitches" 1.5 cm (¹/₂ in) long, using contrasting threads.

9 Draw the legs, beaks and plumes free-hand with a marker pencil.

10 Pin a piece of interfacing to the wrong side of the ground fabric underneath each area to be stitched. Work the legs in satin stitch. ▶

11 Lower the feed on the sewing machine and attach a darning foot. Place the piece in an embroidery hoop and fill in the beak with a wide zigzag stitch at a 45-degree angle. Work the plumes in the same way. Tear away the interfacing from the wrong side.

12 For the eyes, thread a needle with a contrasting thread and hand stitch a button to the centre of each head.

13 For an even blanket stitch along the top and bottom edges of the ground fabric, use a metal rule to mark dots at 1 cm ($^1/_2$ in) intervals, 2.5 cm (1 in) in from the edge.

14 To work the blanket stitch, use hand embroidery thread in a contrasting colour and tack on the thread at one corner. Insert the needle at the first mark, loop the thread under the point of the needle, pull the needle through and insert it at the next mark. Continue in this way along the edge of the fabric.

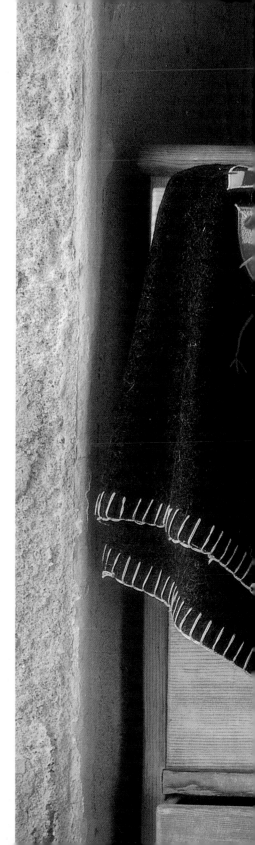

BEADED NECKLACE

THIS STUNNING NECKLACE, DESIGNED BY JUDY CLAYTON, FEATURES A SIMPLE BUT HIGHLY EFFECTIVE EMBROIDERY TECHNIQUE. THE CORDS, WHICH APPEAR TO BE WRAPPED, ARE IN FACT EMBROIDERED. FROM THE DAZZLING RANGE OF BEADS AVAILABLE, JUDY HAS CHOSEN AN UNUSUALLY SHAPED BEAD IN A COLOUR THAT PICKS OUT THE TURQUOISE IN THE STITCHWORK. THE BEADS ARE SUSPENDED BETWEEN THE CORDS ON JEWELLERY WIRE.

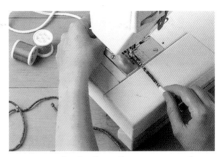

1 Lower the feed on the sewing machine and attach a darning foot. Fill the bobbin with a metallic thread and use a coloured thread on the top. Set a medium to wide zigzag width and feed the cords through several times, changing the colours each time to give a mottled effect. Create bobbles at intervals along the length of the cord by stitching back and forth over a point with metallic thread.

2 Draw four heart templates, approximately 1 cm (1/2 in) tall, on to thin card. Use the template to draw four hearts on a piece of felt and cut them out with sharp embroidery scissors. Pin the hearts on to a piece of water-soluble polythene and place in an embroidery hoop. Set the stitch width to 0 and fill in the shapes with whip stitch, spiralling outwards from the centre to the edge. Immerse the piece in water and pull away the polythene.

3 On a pin board, pin out the shortest length of cord to make the inner ring and the medium length 2 cm (3/4 in) from the first to make the outer ring. Pin the longest length of cord around the outer ring, making curves along its length. Hand stitch the points where the curves meet the outer ring. Using pliers, bind the ends of the cords together with brass jewellery wire. Cut 22 pieces of wire 5 cm (2 in) long and thread a bead on to each one. Using pliers, twist one end of each wire around the inner cord and the other around the outer cord. Attach some of the beaded wires between the curved cord and the outer ring. Trim the ends.

4 Cut four 6 cm (2 1/2 in) lengths of wire. Pierce a hole at the top and bottom of each heart with a needle. Thread each wire through a bead, then through the heart and another bead. Twist each end of the wire into a spiral and attach both ends to the cord. Hand stitch the clasp to the ends of the cords.

MATERIALS AND EQUIPMENT YOU WILL NEED

DARNING FOOT • NEEDLE SIZE 90/14 • FINE METALLIC AND COLOURED MACHINE EMBROIDERY THREADS • THICK CORD, 40 CM (16 IN) AND 72 CM (29 IN) LONG • THIN CORD, 60 CM (24 IN) • THIN CARD • PEN • FELT • EMBROIDERY SCISSORS • PINS • WATER-SOLUBLE POLYTHENE • EMBROIDERY HOOP • PIN BOARD • NEEDLE • JEWELLERY PLIERS • BRASS JEWELLERY WIRE • WIRE CUTTERS • BEADS • CLASP FASTENING

VELVET WRAP

THIS WRAP HAS BEEN PIECED TOGETHER FROM DYED AND APPLIQUÉD PANNÉ VELVET. PANNÉ VELVET HAS A SOFT, SMOOTH APPEARANCE WHICH IS CREATED IN THE MANUFACTURING PROCESS BY FLATTENING THE PILE WITH A HEAVY ROLLER. AS PANNÉ VELVET IS EXPENSIVE, A CHEAPER ALTERNATIVE IS TO BUY VISCOSE VELVET AND PRESS IT FIRMLY ON THE RIGHT SIDE WITH THE IRON SET TO A HIGH TEMPERATURE. THE APPLIQUÉD FABRIC IS A SEMI-TRANSLUCENT SHOT METALLIC ORGANZA. THIS GAUZY CLOTH IS IDEAL FOR APPLIQUÉ AS THE TEXTURE AND COLOUR OF THE GROUND FABRIC ARE SOFTENED THROUGH ITS SUBTLE SHEEN. MAKE YOUR OWN TASSELS TO TRIM THE WRAP AS STORES OFFER ONLY A LIMITED SELECTION — CHOOSE HAND EMBROIDERY THREADS OR METALLIC YARNS.

1 Cut four pieces of velvet 45 x 45 cm (18 x 18 in) and three pieces 45 x 15 cm (18 x 6 in). Dye the larger pieces a dark colour and the smaller pieces a lighter colour, following the manufacturer's instructions. Rinse thoroughly.

2 aWhen dry, press each piece with a hot iron on the right side to create a lustrous sheen.

3 Trace the template from the back of the book, enlarging as required. Trace four templates on to tissue paper.

MATERIALS AND EQUIPMENT YOU WILL NEED

WHITE VELVET, 1.5 M X 90 CM (1½ YD X 36 IN) • DRESSMAKER'S SHEARS • HOT DYES • SALT • IRON • TISSUE PAPER • METALLIC ORGANZA, 1 M X 90 CM (1 YD X 36 IN) • PINS • DARNING FOOT • NEEDLE SIZE 90/14 • EMBROIDERY HOOP • METALLIC AND MATCHING MACHINE EMBROIDERY THREADS • EMBROIDERY SCISSORS • PRESSER FOOT • CARD • SIX SKEINS OF HAND EMBROIDERY THREAD • TAPESTRY NEEDLE • LINING FABRIC, 1.5 M X 90 CM (1½ YD X 36 IN) • NEEDLE • SEWING THREAD

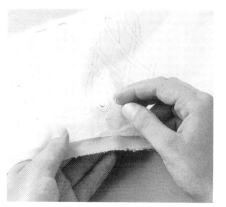

4 Cut three pieces of organza 45 x 15 cm (18 x 6 in). Lay a piece of organza on the right side of each of the smaller pieces of velvet and a tissue paper template on the wrong side, leaving a 2 cm (³/₄ in) seam allowance. Pin the layers together to hold them in place.

5 Lower the feed on the sewing machine and attach a darning foot. Place the piece to be embroidered first in an embroidery hoop, wrong side up. Fill the bobbin with metallic thread and use matching thread on top for a whip stitch. Stitch around the outline.

6 Remove the hoop and trim away the excess organza close to the stitched line using sharp embroidery scissors.

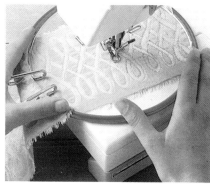

7 Replace the fabric in the hoop, right side up. Fill the bobbin with matching thread and use metallic thread on top. Set a narrow zigzag on the sewing machine width and work along the stitched line, neatening the raw edges.

8 Cut two pieces of organza 45 x 30 cm (18 x 12 in). Lay a piece of organza on the right side of each of two of the larger pieces of velvet close to one edge. Lay a tissue paper template on the wrong side, leaving a 2 cm (³/₄ in) seam allowance. Stitch the design as described in steps five to seven. Raise the feed on the sewing machine, attach a presser foot and choose an appropriate stitch length. Stitch the velvet pieces together along the long edges to make a strip.

▶

9 Cut a piece of card, 7.5 x 7.5 cm (3 x 3 in). For each tassel, wrap one and a half skeins of hand embroidery thread around the card.

11 Bind the tassel 1 cm (¹/₂ in) from the top end and oversew the top.

10 Thread a tapestry needle and backstitch across the top of the tassel. Cut the threads at the other end using sharp scissors.

12 Tear away the tissue paper. Cut a piece of lining to the same size as the velvet piece. With the right sides facing, pin them together. Stitch the seam all around, leaving a 20 cm (8 in) gap on one long edge. Turn the wrap the right way out, turn under the raw edges and slip stitch the gap closed. Stitch a tassel to each corner of the wrap.

SEASHORE SLIPPERS

Lucinda Ganderton has designed these ingenious slippers in cotton waffle-textured fabric, although any heavyweight fabric can be chosen. Covered with delicate seaside motifs, the slippers are trimmed with an art deco wave border. The embroidered motifs are worked on a separate piece of fabric, cut out and applied with a bonding agent and a satin stitch to keep the appliqué crisp. The template is for the left foot and should be reversed to make the right slipper. The piece is worked in a wooden hoop as a spring hoop will not hold such a thick fabric.

1 Trace the template from the back of the book, enlarging as required. Lay a piece of dressmaker's carbon face down between the tracing paper and the cotton drill. Press firmly with a ballpoint pen to transfer the outlines of the motifs. The template is for the left slipper. Turn the tracing over for the right slipper.

2 Lower the feed on the sewing machine and attach a darning foot. Place the fabric in an embroidery hoop. Set a medium zigzag width and fill in the motifs in your chosen colours.

3 To shade the shells, set the stitch width to 0, fill the bobbin with darker thread and use a lighter thread on the top for a whip stitch. Work around the outlines of the shells.

▶

MATERIALS AND EQUIPMENT YOU WILL NEED

Dressmaker's carbon • Small piece of cotton drill fabric • Ballpoint pen • Darning foot • Needle size 90/14 • Embroidery hoop • Coloured machine embroidery threads • Embroidery scissors • Thin card • Cotton waffle fabric, 40 x 40 cm (16 x 16 in) • Fabric glue • Presser foot • Wadding, 25 x 30 cm (10 x 12 in) • Pins • Needle • Tacking thread • Bias binding, 1 m (1 yd) long • Matching sewing thread

4 Cut out the motifs with embroidery scissors close to the stitched edges.

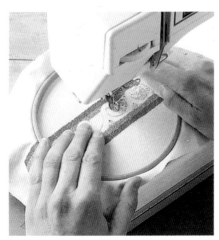

5 Transfer the border pattern to the cotton drill fabric using dressmaker's carbon. Place the piece in an embroidery hoop. Stitch in spiralling motions around the waves, and back and forth over the rest of the design. Cut out the border close to the stitchwork.

6 Make a template from thin card for the upper piece of the slipper. Again, you will need to turn the template over for the right slipper. Cut one piece of cotton waffle fabric for the left slipper and one for the right. Using the template as a guide, glue the border and shells in place. Fold under the straight edge of each piece and glue it down.

7 Raise the feed on the sewing machine and attach a presser foot. Set a medium zigzag width and work a zigzag around each embroidered shape, followed by a satin stitch.

8 Make a template from thin card for the sole, reversing as before for the right slipper. Cut two pieces of cotton waffle fabric and one piece of wadding for each slipper. Lay the wadding between the two layers of fabric and pin all around. Tack and then work a zigzag stitch around the outside edge.

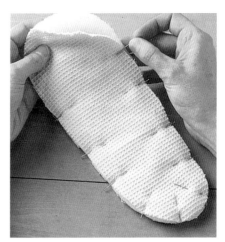

9 Pin and tack each upper piece to a sole. Work a zigzag stitch around the edge. Hand stitch bias binding all around each slipper to enclose the raw edges.

HORSE BROOCH

A THREE-DIMENSIONAL PIECE IN THE SHAPE OF A WINGED HORSE MAKES A STUNNING BROOCH. SUBTLE GLINTS OF LIGHT IN THE EMBROIDERY HINT AT PRECIOUS METAL. THE IMPACT OF THE TEXTURED METALLIC YARN IS TONED DOWN BY THREADING IT THROUGH THE SAME MACHINE NEEDLE AS A PLAIN THREAD IN A HARMONIZING COLOUR. ONCE THE EMBROIDERY IS COMPLETE, THE PIECE IS MANIPULATED BY HAND TO THE DESIRED SHAPE. AN ACRYLIC VARNISH IS APPLIED TO THE WRONG SIDE TO HARDEN THE BROOCH. THE WING TIP IS HIGHLIGHTED WITH A BEADED EDGE. BEADS SHOULD BE STITCHED IN PLACE USING A STRONG THREAD.

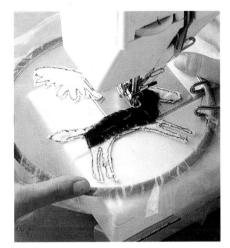

1 Trace the templates from the back of the book, enlarging as required. Cut the horse and wing shapes out of calico and pin them on to a piece of water-soluble polythene.

2 Lower the feed on the sewing machine and attach a darning foot. Place the piece in an embroidery hoop. Stitch around the edges of the shapes. Cut a piece of velvet to the shape of the horse's body. Pin it in place. Fill the bobbin with contrasting thread and use two threads on top, one metallic and one coloured. Stitch over the velvet piece randomly to hold it in place.

3 Fill in the wing area in a contrasting metallic thread. Stitch over the raw edges of each shape in small circular motions to neaten them.

▶

MATERIALS AND EQUIPMENT YOU WILL NEED

CALICO, 20 x 20 CM (8 x 8 IN) • DRESSMAKER'S SHEARS • WATER-SOLUBLE POLYTHENE • PINS • DARNING FOOT • NEEDLE SIZE 90/14 • EMBROIDERY HOOP • SMALL PIECE OF VELVET • METALLIC AND COLOURED MACHINE EMBROIDERY THREADS • CORD • ACRYLIC VARNISH • PAINTBRUSH • BEADING NEEDLE • INVISIBLE THREAD • BEADS • BROOCH BACK • NEEDLE

4 Curve a length of cord around the outline of each shape. Set a medium zigzag width and couch the cord in place.

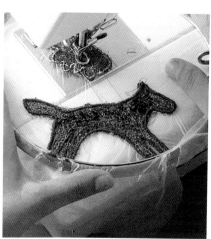

5 Set the stitch width to 0. Work a narrow band inside the couched cord in a contrasting colour.

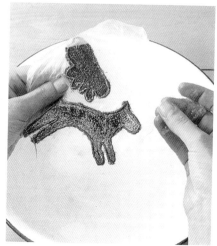

6 Immerse the piece in cold water and pull away the polythene.

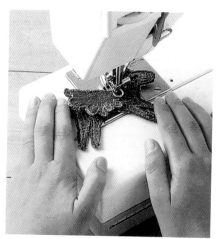

7 Stitch one end of the wing on to the horse's back in a matching colour.

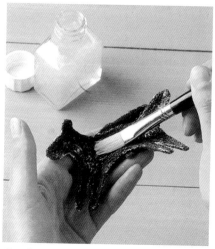

8 Shape the horse and the wing by hand. To secure the shape, paint acrylic varnish on to the wrong side of the pieces. Allow to dry.

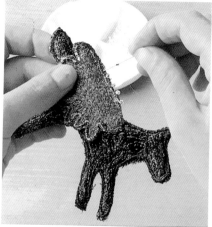

9 Thread a beading needle with invisible thread and stitch small beads around the edges of the wing. Stitch larger beads on to each hoof. Stitch a brooch back on to the wrong side of the piece.

"DIAMOND" EARRINGS

CLARE SOWDEN'S DIAMOND-SHAPED EARRINGS ARE MADE FROM APPLIQUÉD SILK AND ORGANZA PIECES EMBROIDERED IN A COMBINATION OF COLOURS AND TEXTURES TO GIVE A PRECIOUS, JEWEL-LIKE QUALITY. THE APPLIQUÉ SHAPES ARE STUFFED WITH WADDING TO MAKE THE EARRINGS THREE-DIMENSIONAL WHILE REMAINING EXTREMELY LIGHT. CONSIDER OTHER FABRICS FOR MAKING APPLIQUÉD JEWELLERY PIECES, SUCH AS VELVET, SATIN AND SHOT SILKS.

1 Draw two diamond shapes to the required size, and make a template from thin card. Use the template to draw two diamond shapes on the calico. Draw four horizontal lines inside each diamond with a fabric marker or pen. Cut two small pieces of organza slightly larger than the template and pin them over the marked shapes. Lower the feed on the sewing machine and attach a darning foot. Place the fabric in an embroidery hoop. With matching thread, stitch the horizontal lines and several lines around the design. Trim away the excess organza close to the stitched outline.

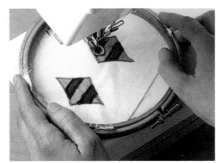

2 Cut two small pieces of silk fabric in a contrasting colour and pin them over the diamond shapes. Place the piece in a hoop and stitch several lines around the horizontal stripes with matching thread. Trim away any excess fabric close to the stitch line. Work several stitch lines around the appliquéd stripes to cover the raw edges.

3 Work more stitch lines around the design with metallic thread.

4 Pin a second piece of calico to the wrong side of the embroidery. Place it in the hoop, and stitch around three sides of each diamond shape. Stuff both shapes with wadding, poking it into the corners. Stitch the fourth side to close the gap. Cut out the shapes close to the stitched outline. With a small brush, apply PVA glue to the edges of the shapes to varnish and stiffen the embroidered piece. Leave to dry, then paint the back and the edges in a metallic acrylic paint. When the paint has dried, make a hole at the top of each diamond with a needle. Thread each eye pin through a small metallic bead, a glass bead and then the diamond. Using jewellery pliers, twist the wire at the back to secure in place and attach the ear wires to the eye pins.

MATERIALS AND EQUIPMENT YOU WILL NEED

THIN CARD • EMBROIDERY SCISSORS • SMALL PIECES OF CALICO • FABRIC MARKER OR PEN • SMALL PIECES OF ORGANZA AND SILK • PINS • DARNING FOOT • NEEDLE SIZE 80/12 • EMBROIDERY HOOP • COLOURED AND METALLIC MACHINE EMBROIDERY THREADS • WADDING • PVA GLUE • PAINTBRUSH • METALLIC ACRYLIC PAINT • NEEDLE • TWO EYE PINS • TWO METALLIC BEADS • TWO GLASS BEADS • JEWELLERY PLIERS • TWO EAR WIRES

CHIFFON SCARF

ABIGAIL MILL HAS CHOSEN A WONDERFUL COMBINATION OF FABRICS FOR THIS UNUSUAL SCARF; SILK AND VELVET ARE SET ON A GROUND OF OLIVE-GREEN CHIFFON, CREATING A PIECE RICH IN TEXTURE, SHAPE AND COLOUR. "SHOT", OR CROSSWOVEN, SILKS HAVE AN IRIDESCENT QUALITY, THE COLOUR APPEARING TO CHANGE WHEN THE CLOTH MOVES. THEIR INCLUSION ADDS DEPTH TO THE APPLIQUÉ AND A FEELING OF RICHNESS TO THE DESIGN. THE CASCADING MULTILAYERED LEAVES AND TROPICAL POD SHAPES ARE LINKED BY A SPIRALLING DESIGN WORKED IN METALLIC THREAD.

1 Draw the leaf and pod shapes freehand. Make templates from thin card. Cut several pieces of fusible interlining and draw around the templates on to the paper backing. Press the fusible interlining to bond it to the wrong side of the appliqué fabrics. Cut out the shapes with embroidery scissors. Remove the paper backing from the appliqué pieces and arrange the shapes at either end of the length of chiffon.

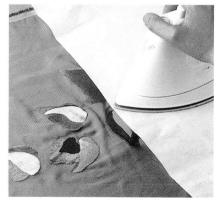

2 Cover the fabric with a sheet of paper and press to bond the appliqué pieces to the chiffon ground fabric.

3 Lower the feed on the sewing machine and attach a darning foot. Place the piece in an embroidery hoop. Fill the bobbin with a coloured thread and use a contrasting metallic thread on top for a whip stitch. Work several lines of stitching around the edges of the appliqué pieces. Stitch spirals and scrolls over the appliqué and ground fabric.

4 To line the scarf, pin and tack the chiffon and organza lengths, right sides together. Raise the feed on the sewing machine and attach a presser foot. Choose an appropriate stitch length and stitch a seam around the edges, leaving a 2 cm (³/₄ in) seam allowance. Leave a gap of 8 cm (3 in) in one of the long sides. Finally, turn the scarf the right way out. Turn under the raw edges and slip stitch the gap closed by hand.

MATERIALS AND EQUIPMENT YOU WILL NEED

THIN CARD • FUSIBLE INTERLINING • EMBROIDERY SCISSORS • IRON •
SMALL PIECES OF METALLIC ORGANZA, SHOT SATIN, VELVET AND CHIFFON • CHIFFON, 36 x 162 CM (14 x 65 IN) • PAPER •
DARNING FOOT • NEEDLE SIZE 80/12 • EMBROIDERY HOOP • METALLIC AND COLOURED MACHINE EMBROIDERY THREADS •
METALLIC ORGANZA, 36 x 162 CM (14 x 65 IN) • NEEDLE • PINS • PRESSER FOOT • MATCHING SEWING THREAD

WOOLLEN HAT

A FRIENDLY DOG CHASES A RUNAWAY KITE THROUGH FLOATING SNOWFLAKES ON THIS WOOLLEN HAT. THE DELIGHTFUL DESIGN IS STITCHED IN MATT WOOLLEN THREADS WHICH CAN BE WORKED IN THE BOBBIN OR THREADED THROUGH A LARGE NEEDLE. AN INLAID APPLIQUÉ TECHNIQUE IS USED TO PRODUCE THE PATCHWORK EFFECT. AREAS OF CLOTH ARE CUT AWAY TO LEAVE NEGATIVE SHAPES, WHICH ARE FILLED WITH POSITIVE SHAPES IN CONTRASTING COLOURS. THIS APPLIQUÉ TECHNIQUE IS BEST SUITED TO FABRICS OF EQUAL THICKNESS AND WHICH ARE NOT PRONE TO FRAYING, SUCH AS NON-WOVEN CLOTHS. TRADITIONALLY, INLAID APPLIQUÉ WAS WORKED WITHOUT A GROUND FABRIC, WHEREAS HERE THE INLAID FABRIC IS TACKED IN PLACE ON A BACKGROUND.

1 Trace the templates from the back of the book, enlarging as required, and make templates from thin card. Fold the woollen ground fabric in half lengthways and mark the fold with pins. Unfold the fabric and lay it flat.

2 Arrange the templates on the length of the fold and draw around them with a fabric marker. Cut out the shapes with embroidery scissors and discard.

3 Draw around the templates on the pieces of contrasting woollen fabric and cut them out. Cut four small triangles

to fit inside the kite shape. Fold the ground fabric in half along the pinned line. Fit the cut-out shapes into the holes in the ground fabric, trimming if required. Pin the shapes in place.

4 Thread a needle and tack the inlaid pieces securely in place. ▶

MATERIALS AND EQUIPMENT YOU WILL NEED
THIN CARD • WOOLLEN FABRIC, 64 X 68 CM (26 X 27 IN) • PINS • FABRIC MARKER • EMBROIDERY SCISSORS •
SMALL PIECES OF CONTRASTING WOOLLEN FABRIC • NEEDLE • TACKING THREAD • DARNING FOOT • NEEDLE SIZE 100/16 •
EMBROIDERY HOOP (OPTIONAL) • WOOLLEN MACHINE EMBROIDERY THREADS • PRESSER FOOT • MATCHING SEWING THREAD

5 Lower the feed on the sewing machine and attach a darning foot. Either place the piece in a wooden embroidery hoop or hold the fabric firmly between your fingers. Stitch a wobbly line around the outlines of the dog and kite shapes in a contrasting woollen thread, using the same thread in both the bobbin and on the top. On each snowflake, stitch a star shape in a contrasting thread.

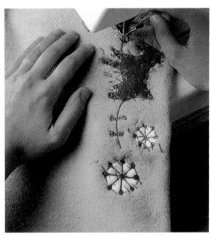

6 Draw the kite tail freehand with a fabric marker, and stitch it.

7 Unfold the piece and pin the two side edges together with the right sides facing. Raise the feed on the sewing machine and attach a presser foot. Stitch the seam, leaving a 2 cm (³/₄ in) seam allowance. Refold the piece with the seam line at the centre back.

8 Fold the embroidered section to the right side. Pin and machine stitch a seam across the top edge of the inside section.

9 To make fabric ties, cut two strips of wool fabric 5 x 25 cm (2 x 10 in). Fold the strips in half lengthways and tuck in and pin a narrow seam allowance. Work a wide zigzag stitch over the long edge and one short edge.

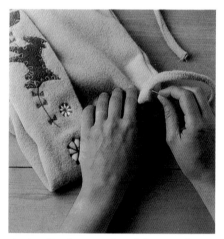

10 On the top edge of the outside section of the hat, fold in a seam allowance and slip stitch the gap closed by hand. Pin the raw end of each tie piece to each corner and stitch in place.

CHILD'S HAT

THIS CHILD'S HAT WAS INSPIRED BY MIRROR AND EMBROIDERY WORK FROM ASIA. THE TINY MIRRORS, KNOWN AS "SHISHA" BY HINDUS AND "ABLAS" BY MUSLIMS, ARE TRADITIONALLY EMBROIDERED ON GARMENTS TO WARD OFF BAD SPIRITS. SUPERSTITION HAS IT THAT MIRRORS TRAP THE EVIL EYE – HOLDING IT IN THEIR REFLECTION FOREVER. USUALLY APPLIED WITH BUTTONHOLE STITCH WORKED BY HAND, MIRRORS CAN ALSO BE TRAPPED BETWEEN LAYERS OF FABRIC AND MACHINE STITCHED IN PLACE. MOTHER-OF-PEARL BUTTONS ADD DECORATIVE DETAIL AND ARE ALSO SAID TO PROTECT THE WEARER FROM EVIL SPIRITS.

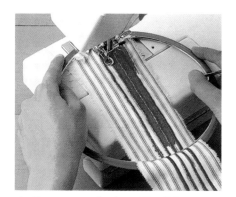

1 Cut a piece of ticking 50 x 7.5 cm (20 x 3 in). Cut a number of lengths of cord 52 cm (21 in) long. Lower the feed on the sewing machine and attach a darning foot. Lay the cords along the stripes of the ticking. Fill the bobbin and the top with contrasting threads for a whip stitch. Set a wide zigzag width and couch each cord in place, changing colours occasionally. Place the piece in an embroidery hoop, set the stitch width to 0 and fill in the stripes between the couching with a whip stitch. Use a different colour for each stripe.

2 Stitch along the long edges using circular motions to neaten them. Make the piece into a band by overlapping the two short edges and stitching back and forth over the join.

3 Cut a piece of ticking 20 x 20 cm (8 x 8 in). Using a pair of compasses, draw a circle with a diameter of 16 cm ($6^{1}/_{4}$ in) for the crown. Draw several concentric circles between the outside edge and the centre. Place the piece in an embroidery hoop. Using contrasting threads in the bobbin and on the top, fill in the rings with whip stitch, changing colours for each ring. Leave the central circle and the outside ring unstitched.

4 Draw small circles at intervals all around the outer ring. Use a whip stitch to fill in the space between the circles. Cut out these circles and the central circle with sharp embroidery scissors.

▶

MATERIALS AND EQUIPMENT YOU WILL NEED
TICKING FABRIC, 50 x 90 CM (20 x 36 IN) • DRESSMAKER'S SHEARS • PIPING CORD •
DARNING FOOT • NEEDLE SIZE 90/14 • COLOURED MACHINE EMBROIDERY THREADS • PAIR OF COMPASSES • MARKER PEN •
EMBROIDERY HOOP • EMBROIDERY SCISSORS • SHISHA MIRRORS • FABRIC GLUE • PINS • MATCHING SEWING THREAD • NEEDLE •
MOTHER-OF-PEARL BUTTONS • CARD • SKEIN OF HAND EMBROIDERY THREAD • TAPESTRY NEEDLE

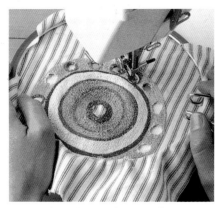

5 Work a whip stitch in circular motions around each circle to neaten all the raw edges.

6 Cut out the embroidered crown and neaten the edge with circular stitching to make a border in a contrasting colour. Cut out pieces of ticking 5 x 5 cm (2 x 2 in). Glue a shisha mirror to the centre of each piece. Pin the patches to the wrong side of the crown all around the outer edge so that each hole is filled with a mirror. Hand stitch the patches in place or work an additional ring of stitching around the inside of the outer ring.

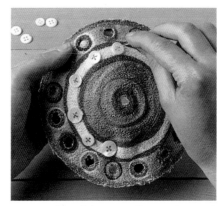

7 Hand stitch buttons all around one of the rings.

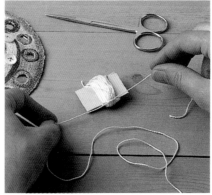

8 To make a pompom, cut a piece of card 5 x 5 cm (2 x 2 in) and wrap the hand embroidery thread evenly around the card. Pass a threaded tapestry needle under the loops at one end and tie them together. Cut the threads at the other end with sharp scissors.

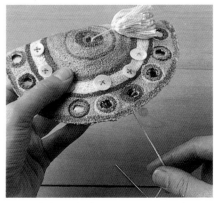

9 Hand stitch the pompom on to the wrong side of the crown so that it protrudes through the central hole on the right side.

10 Hand stitch the crown to the band using a slip stitch.

HARLEQUIN BRACELET

THIS LAVISHLY EMBROIDERED AND DECORATED BRACELET HAS BEEN DESIGNED BY JUDY CLAYTON. THE INTENSELY COLOURED GROUND FABRIC PROVIDES A WONDERFUL CONTRAST TO THE METALLIC STITCHWORK. THE DESIGN IS A STRONG, SIMPLE GEOMETRIC PATTERN REMINISCENT OF SONIA DELAUNAY'S TEXTILES OF THE 1920S. IN THE CENTRE OF EACH DIAMOND SHAPE SITS AN EMBROIDERED DOME ON WHICH BALANCES A SINGLE BEAD.

1 Cut a card template to the size required. Use the template to cut two pieces of silk leaving a 2.5 cm (1 in) seam allowance all around. Draw the pattern on to one piece with a fabric marker. Turn under the seam allowance on both pieces and press.

2 Lower the feed on the sewing machine and attach a darning foot.

Stabilize the piece of silk fabric with the pattern to a piece of fine fabric stabilizer and place in an embroidery hoop. Fill the bobbin with contrasting thread and use a metallic thread on top for a whip stitch. Fill in each diamond and triangle shape in a spiral from the centre to the outside edge. Trim away the fine stabilizing fabric close to the edges of the stitching. Paint the diagonal lines between the stitched areas in a metallic fabric paint. With an iron, press the piece between two sheets of clean white paper to fix the paint.

3 Draw four circles around a small coin on to water-soluble polythene and place it in an embroidery hoop. Use a fine metallic thread on top and fill the bobbin with a coloured thread. Work back and forth from the centre of each circle to the outline. Then work a spiral from the centre to the outline. Immerse the piece in cold water and pull away the polythene. Press each circle into a dome shape.

4 Thread a beading needle with invisible thread and sew a bead to the pinnacle of each dome shape. Stitch each dome at four points around its base to the point where two diamond shapes meet. Cut seven pieces of jewellery wire 10 cm (4 in) long. File the ends and twist a spiral at each end using jewellery pliers. On the sewing machine, set a medium zigzag width. Using metallic thread, couch the wires on to the bracelet, one through each diamond and one at each end of the bracelet. Pin the second piece of silk to the embroidered piece, wrong sides together. Set the stitch width to 0 and work a line of stitching around the edge. Hand stitch a clasp fastening to each end.

MATERIALS AND EQUIPMENT YOU WILL NEED

THIN CARD • SILK, 30 x 30 CM (12 x 12 IN) • DRESSMAKER'S SHEARS • FABRIC MARKER • IRON • DARNING FOOT • NEEDLE SIZE 80/90–12/14 • FINE FABRIC STABILIZER • EMBROIDERY HOOP • METALLIC AND COLOURED MACHINE EMBROIDERY THREADS • EMBROIDERY SCISSORS • METALLIC FABRIC PAINT • PAINTBRUSH • WHITE PAPER • COIN • WATER-SOLUBLE POLYTHENE • BEADING NEEDLE • INVISIBLE THREAD • BEADS • BRASS JEWELLERY WIRE • WIRE CUTTERS • JEWELLERY FILE AND PLIERS • NEEDLE • CLASP FASTENINGS

GLITTERING HAIR COMB

THIS UNUSUAL COMB WITH ITS FAN-SHAPED PIECES IS DECORATED WITH DEEPLY WORKED EMBROIDERY. THERE ARE NO SOLID AREAS OF COLOUR, BUT A DENSELY MOTTLED SURFACE IS CREATED BY WHIP STITCHING ONE COLOUR OVER ANOTHER IN A CIRCULAR MOTION. FOR THIS, THE TENSION OF THE TOP THREAD IS TIGHTENED AND THE BOBBIN THREAD LOOSENED TO BRING THE LOWER THREAD TO THE FRONT OF THE PIECE. FILLING THE BOBBIN WITH CONTRASTING THREAD GIVES A BEADED EFFECT. AREAS ARE STITCHED SO ONE COLOUR DOMINATES BUT THERE ARE NO DEFINING LINES, ONE SHAPE BLENDING INTO THE NEXT.

1 Trace the templates from the back of the book, enlarging as required, and make card or paper templates. Draw around the templates on to the calico, cut out the pieces and pin them on to a piece of water-soluble polythene. Lower the feed on the sewing machine and attach a darning foot. Place the piece in an embroidery hoop. Use contrasting threads in the bobbin and on the top for a whip stitch. Work in circular motions to fill in the outline. Stitch areas of different colours bleeding into each other to give a mottled effect. Stitch in circular motions to neaten the raw edges.

2 Turn the piece wrong side up in the hoop. Fill the bobbin with metallic thread and use contrasting thread on the top. Work a cable stitch along the zigzag edge of the larger piece.

3 Immerse the pieces in cold water and pull away the polythene. Cut a piece of card 2.5 x 2.5 cm (1 x 1 in). Cut eight

1 m (1 yd) lengths of jewellery wire. Wrap a wire around the card. Cut the wire at one end and twist the strands together at the other end to secure the tassel. Make eight tassels. Set a medium zigzag width and, using metallic thread in the bobbin and on the top, couch the tassels in place between the points on the larger piece.

4 Lay the smaller piece on top of the larger, matching up the bottom edges. Set the stitch width to 0 and join the two pieces together in matching thread, using circular motions. Hand stitch the top bar of the comb to the bottom edge of the embroidered piece. Draw around the larger template on to a piece of self-adhesive felt and cut it out. Peel off the paper backing and stick the felt on to the back of the embroidery.

MATERIALS AND EQUIPMENT YOU WILL NEED

THIN CARD OR PAPER • FABRIC MARKER • CALICO, 18 x 18 CM (7 x 7 IN) • EMBROIDERY SCISSORS • WATER-SOLUBLE POLYTHENE • PINS •
DARNING FOOT • NEEDLE SIZE 80/12 • EMBROIDERY HOOP • COLOURED AND THICK METALLIC MACHINE EMBROIDERY THREADS •
BRASS JEWELLERY WIRE • WIRE CUTTERS • HAIR COMB • MATCHING SEWING THREAD • NEEDLE • SELF-ADHESIVE FELT

STARRY CAMISOLE

THE ELEGANCE AND GLAMOUR OF LINGERIE FROM THE 1930S ARE REVIVED IN THIS DELICATE CAMISOLE. THE ICE CREAM-COLOURED BODICE IS ADORNED WITH A FIRMAMENT OF OPEN-WORK STARS. THE STAR SHAPES ARE CUT AWAY, THE RAW EDGES ARE NEATENED WITH SATIN STITCH AND A LACY EMBROIDERED DESIGN IS SUSPENDED WITHIN THE CUT-OUT SHAPE, USING WATER-SOLUBLE POLYTHENE AS A STABILIZER. A SPECIALLY DESIGNED CAMISOLE PATTERN DRAFTED BY THE AUTHOR HAS BEEN USED HERE. EITHER DESIGN YOUR OWN PATTERN OR PURCHASE A COMMERCIAL ONE AND ADAPT THE EMBROIDERED DESIGN TO THE PATTERN PIECES.

1 Pin the camisole pattern pieces on to the satin fabric. Draw around the pattern pieces with fabric marker, marking in the darts. Cut the piece out, leaving a 2 cm (³/₄ in) allowance all around.

2 Trace the template from the back of the book, enlarging as required. Trace the stars on to the pattern pieces, arranging them to avoid darts and placing them no closer than 2.5 cm (1 in) to the seam allowance. To transfer the design to the satin, you can tape the tracing and the satin to a window or light box, or cut out the star shapes in the pattern pieces and mark them on the satin in fabric marker.

3 Cut a piece of water-soluble polythene to the same size as the pattern piece and pin it to the wrong side of the satin fabric. Lower the feed on the sewing machine and attach a darning foot. Place the piece in an embroidery hoop. Fill the bobbin with metallic embroidery thread and use the same on top. Stitch the star outlines.

4 With a pair of sharp embroidery scissors, cut out each star shape inside the outline, close to the stitch line.

5 Set a narrow zigzag width and work around the star shapes to enclose the raw edges.

MATERIALS AND EQUIPMENT YOU WILL NEED

COMMERCIAL CAMISOLE PATTERN • SATIN FABRIC, 2 M X 90 CM (2 YD X 36 IN) • PINS • FABRIC MARKER • DRESSMAKER'S SHEARS •
MASKING TAPE (OPTIONAL) • WATER-SOLUBLE POLYTHENE • DARNING FOOT • NEEDLE SIZE 80/12 • EMBROIDERY HOOP •
METALLIC AND CONTRASTING MACHINE EMBROIDERY THREADS • EMBROIDERY SCISSORS • THIN CARD • PAPER SCISSORS •
PAIR OF COMPASSES AND PENCIL • PRESSER FOOT • MATCHING SEWING THREAD • NEEDLE • CONTRASTING RIBBON

6 Set a medium zigzag width and work a satin stitch around the stars.

7 Work a straight stitch across the water-soluble polythene from each star point to its centre. Stitch a spiral from the centre outwards to make a small circle. Stitch "veins" from the radiating lines to the outline. At each point, stitch a small splayed fringe.

8 Remove the fabric from the hoop and draw the looping lines and smaller stars freehand. Set the stitch width to 0 and fill in the small stars. Stitch a single line of embroidery between them along the looping lines.

9 To make a template for the scalloped edge, cut a piece of card 12.5 x 5 cm (5 x 2 in). Draw a line to divide the card in half lengthways. Draw semi circles along the pencil line with a pair of compasses set at a radius of 2.5 cm (1 in). Cut out the template using paper scissors.

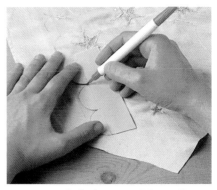

10 Match the bottom of the scallops to the seam line, starting at the top point of the satin. Draw around the scallops with a fabric marker, rounding off the curve at the top freehand.

11 Cut a piece of water-soluble polythene and pin it to the wrong side of the satin. Place the piece in an embroidery hoop. Work a line of stitching around the scallops in contrasting thread. ▶

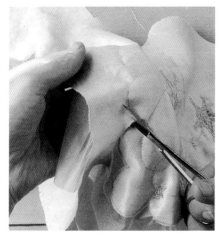

12 Using sharp embroidery scissors, trim away the excess satin fabric close to the stitch line.

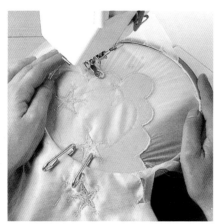

13 Place the satin and polythene in an embroidery hoop. Set a narrow zigzag width and work around the scallops to enclose all the raw edges. Set a medium stitch width and work a satin stitch around the scallops.

14 Immerse the piece in cold water and pull away the polythene from the embroidery. Raise the feed on the sewing machine and attach a presser foot. Make up the camisole according to the manufacturer's instructions using matching sewing thread.

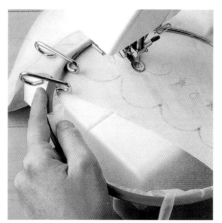

15 Around the hem, draw and stitch small stars and looping lines. Draw and stitch a scalloped edge as described above. For the shoulder straps, hand stitch a length of ribbon on each side.

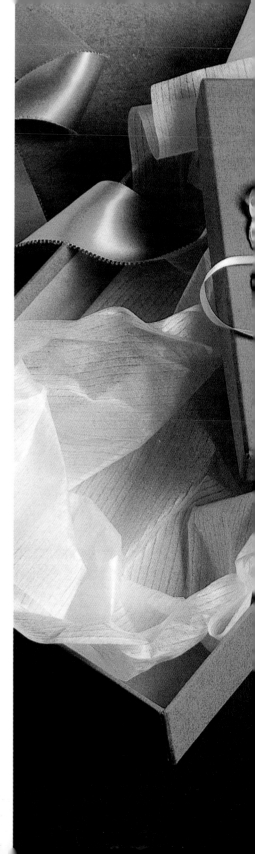

ANGEL DECORATION

STARS DANCE IN THE HAIR AND ARE SUSPENDED BENEATH THIS UNUSUAL ANGEL DECORATION. SHE CAN BE HUNG ON A CHRISTMAS TREE OR A MANTELPIECE. THE FACE AND NOSE AREAS ARE RAISED IN RELIEF BY SHAPING AND STITCHING ON THE WRONG SIDE. THE FACE IS SHADED USING A DARKER THREAD IN THE BOBBIN FOR A WHIP STITCH, TO CREATE SUBTLE SHADOWS. THE HAIR AND THE WINGS ARE WORKED IN LUSTROUS FLOSS THREAD, WHICH CAN ONLY BE USED IN THE BOBBIN. UNUSUAL THREADS ARE COUCHED IN PLACE BY HAND TO HIGHLIGHT DETAILS AND GIVE THE PIECE A THREE-DIMENSIONAL APPEARANCE.

1 Trace the templates for the head and wings from the back of the book, enlarging as required. Cut out the shapes from calico. Draw the details freehand in fabric marker. Lower the feed on the sewing machine and attach a darning foot. Pin the head piece to a piece of polythene and place it in an embroidery hoop. Fill the bobbin with a light-coloured thread and use a darker thread on the top for a whip stitch. Work several lines of stitching around the features. Fill in the face, lips and eyelids with areas of solid stitchwork in appropriate colours, using whip stitch to shade areas of the face. Stitch around the outline of the face in a contrasting colour, working in circular motions over the edge of the face to neaten the raw edges.

2 To stitch the hair, turn the piece wrong side up in the hoop. Fill the bobbin with a black floss thread and use a matching coloured thread on the top. Work wavy lines from the centre parting to the ends of the hair in cable stitch.

3 Turn the piece right side up in the hoop. Using black thread in the

bobbin and metallic textured thread on the top, fill in the gaps between the strands of hair and highlight the lips and eyelids. Neaten the raw edges around the hair outline by stitching in circular motions. Stitch stars over the hair using a fine metallic thread.

4 Immerse the piece in a bowl of water and pull away the polythene. To produce raised areas, thread a needle and pinch the nose lengthways. On the wrong side, hand stitch back and forth from one side of the nose to the other, pulling gently to raise the area on the right side. Stitch back and forth across the length of the face, pulling slightly, and secure the thread. Stitch back and forth across the width of the face and all around the hair in the same way. ▶

MATERIALS AND EQUIPMENT YOU WILL NEED

CALICO, 20 x 20 CM (8 x 8 IN) • DRESSMAKER'S SHEARS • FABRIC MARKER • DARNING FOOT • NEEDLE SIZE 90/14 • PINS • WATER-SOLUBLE POLYTHENE • EMBROIDERY HOOP • COLOURED, METALLIC TEXTURED AND PLAIN MACHINE EMBROIDERY THREADS • COLOURED FLOSS • NEEDLE • METALLIC COILED HAND EMBROIDERY THREAD • PIPING CORD • LUREX CHENILLE • MATCHING SEWING THREAD

5 Pin the wing shape to a piece of polythene. Place it wrong side up in an embroidery hoop. Fill the bobbin with a floss thread and use a matching thread on the top for a cable stitch. Fill in the feather shapes across each wing, leaving the central area unstitched. Fill the bobbin with a thick metallic thread to work around the feather shapes and the outline of the wings.

6 Turn the piece right side up in the hoop and place the raised face piece over the unstitched area. Using matching thread, stitch around the edge of the hair in circular motions to join it to the wings. Immerse the piece in a bowl of water and pull away the polythene.

7 Loop the coiled hand embroidery thread over the hair and hand stitch in place using matching thread.

8 Place a piece of polythene in the embroidery hoop and draw star shapes on the polythene in fabric marker. Using a fine metallic thread in the bobbin and on the top, fill in the star shapes by stitching in circular motions, then work back and forth from the centre point to the outline. Stitch several individual stars and one or two strings of stars joined at the points.

9 Set a wide zigzag width and fill the bobbin and the top with different colours of metallic thread for a whip stitch. Feed the piping cord through several times, changing the colours each time to give a mottled effect. Cut the cord into 15 cm (6 in) lengths. Set a medium zigzag width, place one end of each cord on a star and stitch in place.

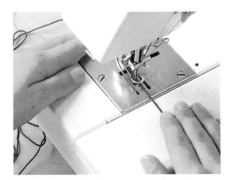

10 Immerse the piece in a bowl of cold water and pull away the polythene. Pin the plain end of each cord to the bottom of the face. Set the stitch width to 0 and stitch the cords in place using a matching thread. Cut a piece of lurex chenille. Make a hoop for hanging and pin the ends to the top of the piece. Hand stitch in place.

EVENING POUCH

THIS UNIQUE AND DELICATE POUCH IS THE WORK OF JUDY CLAYTON. A PIECE OF ART IN ITS OWN RIGHT, IT COULD ADORN A DRESSING TABLE OR BE DISPLAYED IN A CABINET. THE RICH AND IRIDESCENT COLOURS ARE REMINISCENT OF A PEACOCK'S TAIL FEATHERS. THE SHADOW APPLIQUÉ ON THE LID PIECE IS MADE BY APPLYING CUT PIECES OF VELVET TO A GROUND FABRIC. A LAYER OF METALLIC ORGANZA IS LAID ON TOP AND STITCHED IN PATTERNS THAT MIMIC THE SHAPES BENEATH. PARTS OF THE PATTERN HAVE BEEN CUT AWAY TO REVEAL THE CONTRASTING TEXTURE AND COLOUR BENEATH, AND SO CREATE A DISTRESSED EFFECT.

1 Trace the template for the side pieces from the back of the book, enlarging as required, and make a template from thin card. Use the template to cut four pieces of heavyweight interfacing and four pieces of silk. Cut four pieces of metallic organza, leaving a 1 cm ($^1/_2$ in) allowance all around. Place each piece of silk between a piece of interfacing and a piece of metallic organza. Cut thin strips of fusible interlining and press with an iron to bond in place around the edges of the interfacing. Remove the paper backing, fold over the organza edges and press to bond in place.

2 Trace the triangle shape from the back of the book, enlarging as required, and make a template from thin card. Use the template to draw four triangles on to the paper backing of a piece of fusible interlining. Press with an iron to bond the interlining to the wrong side of a piece of velvet. Cut out and remove the paper backing. Press each piece to bond it to the centre of each side piece. Lower the feed on the sewing machine and attach a darning foot. Fill the bobbin with a coloured floss thread and use a contrasting metallic thread on top for a whip stitch. Work several lines of stitching around the edges of each appliqué shape. Work spirals across the centre.

3 Trace the lid template from the back of the book, enlarging as required, and make a template from thin card. Use the template to cut a piece of interfacing and a piece of silk. Cut a piece of metallic organza, leaving a 2 cm ($^3/_4$ in) allowance all around. Position the silk piece on the interfacing. Bond a piece of fusible interlining by pressing it to the wrong side of a piece of velvet. Cut five small, round pieces from the velvet, peel away the paper backing and bond in place on the top of the lid. Lay the metallic organza piece on top of the lid, over the velvet circles, and bond in place as before.

▶

MATERIALS AND EQUIPMENT YOU WILL NEED
THIN CARD • NON-WOVEN HEAVYWEIGHT INTERFACING, 24 x 90 CM (10 x 36 IN) • DRESSMAKER'S SHEARS •
SILK FABRIC, 50 x 90 CM (20 x 36 IN) • TWO COLOURS OF METALLIC ORGANZA, 24 x 90 CM (10 x 36 IN) • FUSIBLE INTERLINING • IRON •
SMALL PIECES OF VELVET • DARNING FOOT • NEEDLE SIZE 80/12 • COLOURED FLOSS AND FINE METALLIC MACHINE EMBROIDERY THREADS •
EMBROIDERY SCISSORS • LINING FABRIC, 25 x 90 CM (10 x 36 IN) • PINS • MATCHING SEWING THREAD • NEEDLE • ARTIFICIAL BONING • CORD

4 Whip stitch in contrasting threads, working spirals and diamonds all over the lid piece. Change the colours several times as you progress.

5 Using sharp embroidery scissors, slash and cut away areas of the organza between the stitching. Work more spirals and diamonds over the cut-work.

6 Use the template to cut another lid piece from the interfacing. Cut one piece of metallic organza and one of lining fabric, leaving a 1 cm (1/2 in) allowance all around. Cut thin strips of fusible interlining and bond the metallic fabric in place on the interfacing. To line the lower lid, lay the lining fabric over the interfacing and press under the turning allowance. Cut strips of fusible interlining, press and fuse in place around the edge of the lid on the wrong side. Remove the paper backing, press and bond the lining in place. Pinch each corner together and work circular stitches over the edges, so that the centre of the lid is pushed out.

7 Pin the embroidered lid to the lower lid on the cross so that they form an eight-pointed star. Hand stitch in place at each corner.

8 To line the side pieces, use the side template to cut four pieces of lining fabric, leaving a 1 cm (1/2 in) allowance all around. Turn over the allowance and press down. Cut thin strips of fusible interlining and press to bond in place around the edges of each piece on the wrong side. Remove the paper backing and bond the lining on to the side pieces. On the sewing machine, set a wide zigzag width and stitch the side seams with the wrong sides facing. Push in the sides, flatten the front and back and stitch the bottom seam. For the handle, fold a piece of lining fabric over a length of boning and stitch in place along its length. Hand stitch the ends to the side pieces of the pouch, 2.5 cm (1 in) from the top edge.

9 Hand stitch one point of the lid to the back of the bag. Decorate the lid with couched cord (see the Beaded Necklace or Angel Decoration projects).

HEART HAT PIN

THE HEART IS A TIMELESS JEWELLERY MOTIF, A SYMBOL EVOKING LOVE AND FRIENDSHIP. THIS DELICATE FILIGREE HAT PIN, WHICH CAN ALSO BE WORN AS A LAPEL PIN, WAS INSPIRED BY BAROQUE GILDING FOUND IN A CZECH CHURCH. A DEGREE OF EXPERTISE IS REQUIRED FOR THE PROJECT AND THE TENSION ON THE SEWING MACHINE SHOULD BE CAREFULLY BALANCED TO AVOID TEARING THE GROUND FABRIC OF WATER-SOLUBLE POLYTHENE.

1 Trace the template from the back of the book, enlarging as required. Lay a piece of polythene over the template and trace the design with a fabric marker. Lower the feed on the sewing machine and attach a darning foot. Place the piece in an embroidery hoop. Using metallic thread, stitch around the lines of the heart motif. Fill in the filigree outline, stitching in small circular motions.

2 Stitch back and forth several times over the circular stitchwork. Turn the piece the other way up in the hoop.

3 Set a narrow zigzag width. Curve a length of jewellery wire around the stitched outline of the heart, starting and finishing at the point. Couch in place. Trim the ends of the wire.

4 Remove the piece from the hoop. Lay the hat pin in the centre of the heart. Set a medium zigzag width and couch the pin in place.

5 Immerse the piece in cold water and pull away the polythene. Using a beading needle and invisible thread, stitch the beads around the edge of the filigree piece. Sew through a large bead, then a small one and back through the large bead. Make a stitch at the edge to secure the beads in place.

MATERIALS AND EQUIPMENT YOU WILL NEED

WATER-SOLUBLE POLYTHENE • FABRIC MARKER • DARNING FOOT • NEEDLE SIZE 70/10–80/12 • EMBROIDERY HOOP •
METALLIC MACHINE EMBROIDERY THREAD • THIN JEWELLERY WIRE • WIRE CUTTERS • HAT PIN • BEADING NEEDLE •
INVISIBLE THREAD • PLASTIC BEADS IN TWO SIZES

DAISY WASH BAG

POLYVINYL CHLORIDE MAY NOT BE THE FIRST FABRIC THAT COMES TO MIND WHEN PLANNING A PIECE OF EMBROIDERY. HOWEVER, ITS QUALITIES OF WATER-REPELLENCE, STRENGTH AND TRANSPARENCY ARE PERFECT FOR A WASH BAG. AS PVC IS A NON-FRAYING MATERIAL, IT CAN BE APPLIQUÉD WITH A SINGLE LINE OF STITCHING. THERE IS NO NEED TO USE A FUSIBLE INTERLINING OR PINS — MASKING TAPE WILL HOLD THE PIECE TO BE APPLIED AND THE TEMPLATE IN PLACE.

1 Trace the template from the back of the book twice, enlarging as required on to tissue paper. Match up the 62 cm (25 in) edges of the polythene and PVC and tape together. Tape the templates side by side on the polythene, leaving a gap at each side and along the bottom edge.

2 Lower the feed on the sewing machine and attach a darning foot. Stitch over the lines of the design, gripping the fabric firmly. Cut away the excess polythene close to the stitched line. Tear away the tissue paper.

3 Turn the piece right side up. Remove the stems and centres from the fabric flowers and leaves. Arrange the flowers within the rings of the design and randomly over the ground fabric. Using contrasting threads in the bobbin and the top for a whip stitch, work radiating lines over the flowers and veins of the leaves.

4 Set a wide zigzag width and work a satin stitch bobble in the centre of each flower.

5 Raise the feed on the sewing machine and attach a presser foot. Choose an appropriate stitch length. Fold the PVC in half widthways, right sides together, and stitch a seam to make a tube. Fold over the embroidered section to the right side. With a pair of compasses, draw and cut out a circle with a 10 cm (4 in) radius on a spare piece of PVC. With right sides together, stitch the circle to the bottom edges of the bag. Across the top folded edge of the bag, mark points at even intervals 2.5 cm (1 in) from the edge. Attach the eyelets following the manufacturer's instructions.

MATERIALS AND EQUIPMENT YOU WILL NEED

TISSUE PAPER • METALLIC POLYTHENE, 62 x 20 CM (25 x 8 IN) • TRANSPARENT PVC, 62 x 90 CM (25 x 36 IN) • MASKING TAPE • DARNING FOOT • NEEDLE SIZE 90/14 • MACHINE EMBROIDERY THREADS • EMBROIDERY SCISSORS • FABRIC FLOWERS • PRESSER FOOT • PAIR OF COMPASSES AND PENCIL • EYELET KIT • SMALL HAMMER

INDIAN-STYLE SILK SQUARE

THE NIGHT BEFORE HER WEDDING, AN INDIAN BRIDE'S PALMS ARE HENNAED IN INTRICATE DESIGNS. THESE DECORATIONS ARE THE INSPIRATION FOR THIS BOLD HAND MOTIF. THE HAND IS PAINTED ON TO A SMOOTH-TEXTURED SILK FABRIC IN SPECIALIZED SILK PAINTS. THESE PAINTS CAN BE MIXED AND WATERED DOWN SO THAT ONLY THE THREE PRIMARY COLOURS AND WHITE ARE NEEDED TO MAKE A NUMBER OF SHADES.

1 Fill a bowl with boiling water. Dissolve four tablespoons of salt and immerse two tea bags in the water. Remove the tea bags and immerse the silk in the tea for ten minutes. Remove the fabric, rinse and press. Trace the template from the back of the book, enlarging as required. Stretch the silk over the template and tape it down. Trace the design with a fabric marker. If you want to repeat the design, draw a grid using the grain of the fabric as a guide and rotate the design 90 degrees each time. Stretch the fabric over the wooden frame, using a hammer and pins to secure it. Ensure that the fabric is taut and that it has no wrinkles.

2 Fill the gutta dispenser with gutta and apply it along the lines of the design. When the gutta is completely dry, pour the silk paints into the palette compartments. Dot a little paint into the centre of each area to be coloured and it will quickly spread to the gutta outline. Apply a wash of colour to the palm area. While the paint is still wet, drop a teaspoon of salt into the centre. Allow the paint to dry, then brush away the salt grains. Remove the silk from the frame and lay it between two sheets of white paper. Press with an iron to fix the paint. Wash the fabric to remove the gutta. Then draw star motifs freehand on the ground fabric with a fabric marker.

3 Lower the feed on the sewing machine and attach a darning foot. Place the fabric in an embroidery hoop and stitch the stars in matching thread.

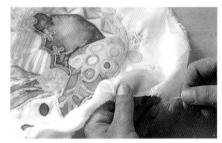

4 Draw additional circles to overlap the painted ones. Fill in the circles in contrasting threads, working a spiral from the centre to the outline. Stitch two or three lines around the palm area, working small bobbles at intervals. Cut away the excess fabric to within 5 cm (2 in) of the edge of the design. Pull away the warp and weft threads around the edges to make a fringe and hand stitch to secure.

MATERIALS AND EQUIPMENT YOU WILL NEED

BOWL • SALT • TWO TEA BAGS • SILK HABOTAI, 1 M X 90 CM (1 YD X 36 IN) • MASKING TAPE • IRON • FABRIC MARKER • WOODEN FRAME • SMALL HAMMER • PINS • GUTTA AND DISPENSER • SILK PAINTS AND PALETTE • PAINTBRUSH • WHITE PAPER • DARNING FOOT • NEEDLE SIZE 90/14 • EMBROIDERY HOOP • MACHINE EMBROIDERY THREADS • MATCHING SEWING THREAD • NEEDLE

TEMPLATES

IF THE TEMPLATES NEED TO BE ENLARGED, EITHER USE A GRID SYSTEM OR A PHOTOCOPIER. FOR THE GRID SYSTEM, TRACE THE TEMPLATE AND DRAW A GRID OF EVENLY SPACED SQUARES OVER YOUR TRACING. TO SCALE UP, DRAW A LARGE GRID ON TO ANOTHER PIECE OF PAPER. COPY THE OUTLINE ON TO THE SECOND SQUARE, TAKING EACH SQUARE INDIVIDUALLY AND DRAWING THE RELEVANT PART OF THE OUTLINE IN THE LARGER SQUARE. FINALLY, DRAW OVER THE LINES TO MAKE SURE THEY ARE CONTINUOUS. ALTERNATIVELY, TWO DIFFERENT SIZES OF GRAPH PAPER MAY BE USED.

SHADOW APPLIQUÉ SHIRT PP35–37

SHADOW APPLIQUÉ SHIRT
PP35–37

APPLIQUÉD NAPKINS
PP28–29

LINEN WAISTCOAT PP32-34

HORSE BROOCH
PP59–61

PAPER PORTFOLIO
PP38—39

KIMONO
PP42—43

CHILD'S BLANKET
PP46—49

▶

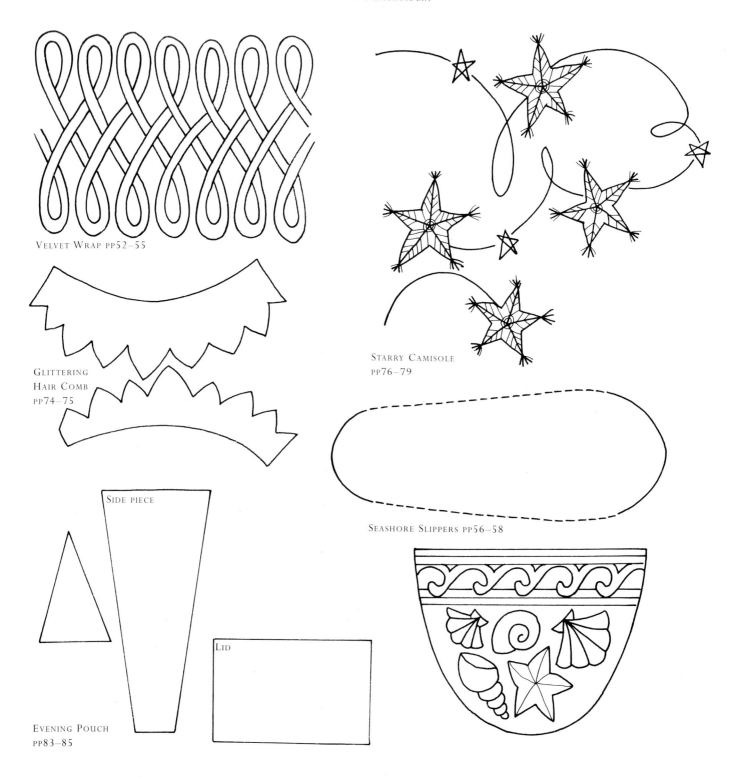

Velvet Wrap pp52–55

Glittering
Hair Comb
pp74–75

Starry Camisole
pp76–79

Seashore Slippers pp56–58

Side piece

Lid

Evening Pouch
pp83–85

WOOLLEN HAT PP66–68

HEART HAT PIN
PP86–87

ANGEL DECORATION PP80–82

INDIAN-STYLE SILK SQUARE PP90–91

DAISY WASH BAG PP88–89

INDEX

SUPPLIERS

United Kingdom

John Lewis
(consult your telephone
directory for nearest branch)
*wide range of sewing equipment
and materials, fabrics and
sewing machines*

Silken Strands
33 Links Way
Gatelly, Cheedle
Cheshire, SK8 4LA
*machine embroidery threads,
available mail order*

Canada

Dressew
337 W Hastings Street
Vancouver, BC
682 6196
sewing and craft materials

Australia

Lincraft
(stores in every capital
city except Darwin). For store
addresses telephone
(03) 9875 7575

Spotlight
(60 stores throughout)
telephone freecall
1800 500 021